Praise for *Selling in an Anxious World . . .*

"Jim Holden is not only a brilliant seller, he is a gifted architect of high performing teams that deliver beyond expectations. *Selling in an Anxious World* is a masterpiece of groundbreaking research and recommendations. To any professional who aspires to greatness, this is a must-read!"

—Bill McDermott
CEO, ServiceNow

"The Holden process for selling has become a bedrock of our company. The fundamentals of Value + Recognition = Power and navigating the customer's political landscape to find the Fox are key elements of our sales success. This book takes the Holden methodology to the next level by highlighting the critical importance of understanding the culture a company builds to support selling. As a Mount Rainier climber myself, I appreciate the analogy of respecting the mountain just like we must respect our customer's environment by listening and employing empathy to really understand that environment, as a key part of the selling process."

—Tom Perlitz
CEO, Ensign-Bickford Industries

"The world has changed. We now live in a gig culture and companies are not what they used to be. In gig culture, people need to be able to move whenever a gig is present. There is no tomorrow. Any doubt and you're out. It's become more about managing the optics of shared calendars than real productivity. Better to lose a deal than lose your

job. As a simple example, in today's company culture, five superficial sales calls per week are more valued than two with substance. This must change." Jim Holden wants to show the reader *"how to think differently about culture, how to create a new sales effectiveness narrative that looks at corporate culture, and how to drive higher levels of professional and personal success. At the same time, building a personal sales philosophy, as 'no real good can happen* through *you until it first happens* to *you.'"*

"*Selling in an Anxious World* presents examples of well-intended, yet counterproductive cultural norms that negatively impact sales. Often driven top-down and technology enabled, most of us will recognize the effects of these norms, complete with the actions of Foxes and Jackals. In many companies, sales performance is being redefined to support the growth strategy, ironically leading to a decline in effectiveness because measurable activity and compliance is often confused with real progress. There is a growing conflict between the sales-averse Looking Glass Culture and winning important deals. Holden adds many personal anecdotes to illustrate the messages. Fortunately, sales is in the perfect position to change culture and make a difference.

"Holden provides actionable guidance to executives, sales managers, and sellers on how to create awareness and bridge the gap between buyers and sellers and between internal, culture-centric and external, client-centric focus in this rapidly changing world. He challenges readers to think about how to be *part of* a culture without being *controlled by* the culture, using the right mix of sensitivity, respect, conviction, and boldness.

"This book made me think about the many different cultures in the companies that I've seen over the years, and about how they impact people's behavior. It presents an interesting way of looking at changes in company cultures that help give a better understanding of how to be successful in selling in this new "gig culture," for example, how to avoid a "Monkey Dance" and keep the focus on your sales objective. Successful sellers will be those who have developed the skills—or entrepreneurship—to really understand both the client and their own company culture, use the cultural overlap to advance their sales objective, and, with executive support, find ways to work around cultural problems when needed to keep their focus on winning deals.

"By the way, adding the Chapter Overview and Quick Reference is a brilliant way of summarizing the book and its key messages."

—Tom Hoppenbrouwer,

Projects & Operations Lead,

Group Sales, Capgemini

"As I read Jim's book, I think he is on to some really important ideas about what is plaguing business, particularly in the United States, today. There is a tension/conflict between the cultures that grow up around pursuing profitable growth organically through product leadership, customer intimacy, and operational excellence, and those that grow up around pursuing profitable growth through mergers and acquisitions. *Selling in an Anxious World* provides a deep-dive into this story.

"As much as executives give lip-service to needing to support both organic and strategic growth strategies, the big-hit wins that come from significant acquisitions often drive stock prices and executive compensation in the short term. They also tend to dominate corporate board rooms (and therefore culture), rather than the relentless pursuit to improve customer satisfaction that is required for successful organic growth. Of course, only a small percentage of acquisitions are truly successful over the long run, and the capital that is required to acquire incremental EBITDA is significantly higher that what is required to grow it organically, but it comes faster. I would also argue that the management and leadership skills needed to "do deals" is significantly lower and more common than that which is required to build and lead a team that consistently delights their customers and 'wins' in the competitive marketplace."

—Jeff Porter
President & CEO, Velvac, Inc.

"What resonates in *Selling in an Anxious World* is Holden's recognition of the negative impact of hyperactivity on sales effectiveness. Today's complex operational demands are distracting salespeople from spending time with their customers. We want sellers to know customers better than the competition does, so we can help them solve their biggest problems. The question is how do we foster a sales culture that puts customers first and frees up seller time for thoughtful preparation that produces effective conversations? These are among the biggest problems facing sales leaders today, and the company that can solve them will win. This book provides solutions!"

—John Borta
Senior Director, Leadership Effectiveness
W.W. Grainger, Inc.

"*Selling in an Anxious World* provides a deep dive analysis into the emerging trend of risk-averse corporate cultures that are driving down sales effectiveness and damaging seller and buyer relationships. This culture-induced anxiety perpetuates an inward-company focus that is harmful to productivity, innovation, and customer centricity that is at the heart of growth. Holden provides a diagnostic approach for assessing culture, and provides a toolbox of strategies for transforming an inward-focused Looking Glass Culture to a Client-Centric Culture that drives company growth and advances sales careers."

—Kevin Nowak

Contractor Vice President,

US Department of Energy

"*Selling in an Anxious World* is very timely—to give the responsibility and accountability of sales back to the account managers. In the last years we have equipped them with professional sales tools, such as CRM and accounts plans, set up funnel management and regular account reviews, as well as controlling pricing very tightly with pricing tools. All of this is very important, as it supports revenue generation, but it can also end up being a 'tick the boxes' exercise.

"In a Looking Glass Culture, internal activity with high tool use and scores is more important, and certainly less risky, than having high scores with customers. We have to tell our account managers that they are best suited to drive a Client-Centric Culture in the company and even more, it is part of their job profile to push for a customer centric culture. But it is also very timely to tell executive management that sponsoring account managers does not mean pushing their own opinions on them. It means getting the best out of people through empowerment that challenges and fosters an environment where anxiety has no place. Avoiding inefficient Monkey Dances is primarily a management responsibility. Thanks, Holden Team, for reminding us of the importance of a Client-Centric Culture and the pitfalls in getting there!"

—Dr. Klemens Brunner

President, Heraeus Electronics

"This book, in its direct and simplistic approach, not only roars a warning about how unnoticed and quietly you, as a salesperson, may drift into an inward-company focus, like the boiling frog, but also provides measures to pave the way out of potential misery. It's a must read for all top management and sales directors, to warn of the clear and present danger of a Looking Glass Culture, if not decisively counteracted."

—Jan Erik Norli

Chief Marketing Officer,

Telenor Maritime

"We are all aware of the maxim, 'Don't judge a book by its cover.' I think in this case, one might alter it to, 'Don't judge a book by its title.' The title is clear and describes the book well, taking a powerful look at sales to create greater success, but it is far more than that. The ideas in *Selling in an Anxious World* are about creating a new point of view, a new process, and a new set of solutions for all types of multifaceted problems, from sales to mountain climbing to medicine. And the author uses real-life stories and analogies that can help any reader understand and experience a new phenomenon in sales, business, and life itself. This book is approachable, educational, eye-opening and engaging.

"As a healthcare provider and biotech executive focused on curing rare diseases, I found great value in this book, even though I would not have thought of myself as a 'sales-focused' businessperson. While reading this book, I realized that the culture issues the author describes were particularly relevant to our company and the many companies and non-profit organizations we work with, or might work with in the future. It opened my eyes to ways I could help myself and my company improve our success rates, and evaluate whether we were likely to have success with current and potential collaborating companies.

"I can also see how these same perspectives, insights, and tools might be useful in solving health issues, whether it involves understanding, preventing, diagnosing, or treating a common or rare disease, managing global public health issues, or helping one patient. Assessing and changing culture, creating alignment among stakeholders, putting the customer/patient first, identifying and leveraging the key individuals who can make or break a decision, and many more ideas presented in this book can help an individual, a team, a company or a nation be more successful.

"And these ideas and tools can be applied right away—there is no long learning curve or huge trial-and-error period. While most of this information was new to me, it is easy to understand and makes good sense. The author provides plenty of support with real-world examples relevant to everyone, even those not primarily in sales.

"The book is organized well, with a clear introduction to let the reader know what to expect, well-written chapters and chapter summaries, and, in the last chapter, a powerful 7-step guide to improving sales success that brings all of the information in the book together. After reading *Selling in an Anxious World*, I am both calmer and more focused about key work issues, and I believe I would both enjoy and feel secure if I were to go mountain climbing, help solve cancer, or improve our company's sales success with Jim Holden."

—Dr. Bruce E. Bloom
Chief Collaboration Officer, Healx

Jim Holden proves, yet again, that he's got his finger on the pulse. *Selling in an Anxious World* provides a great commentary on the changing climate within companies and gives sellers a practical guide on how to navigate the shift. His personal and professional examples paint a vivid picture of what to do and what not to do when selling. A must read for everyone that even touches the sales environment.

—Ewa Washburn
Director of Marketing, Buildout

"*Selling in an Anxious World* is the evolution of Holden's bestselling books with perfect timing for sellers, sales managers, and company executives working in this ever-changing world and economy.

"As a Sales Leader, I know firsthand the impact that *Power Base Selling*, *The New Power Base Selling*, and *The Selling Fox* had on my teams, and I will be delighted to include this new book in our best practice tool-kit.

"Reading *Selling in an Anxious World* expressed what my sales team and I experienced firsthand. At the time, we were not aware we were experiencing a phenomenon that others experienced as well and how it all relates to a gig culture that gives way to the Looking Glass Culture. My sales team is proof you can identify a specific group of customers or a specific solution and create a Client-Centric Culture within a Looking Glass Culture. We had a winning Client-Centric Culture that lasted many years, with the pinnacle of our achievements being when most of the team went to Winner's Circle one year. We always had that executive sponsor that supported us through many a Monkey Dance, but in the end when the company wanted to integrate our team into the regional sales teams, the culture was lost. Today, my sales team members are in other groups, sales teams, and companies, and they all remember how empowered, happy, and joyful they were in our Client-Centric Culture, and they are all working to bring that to where they are today. I was so happy to read how Jim put a name and meaning to everything we experienced!

"*Selling in an Anxious World* takes us on a journey to decipher the ever-changing world through insightful personal stories, the examination of our global economy, and the ever-present change in how we show up as sales professionals. He examines key themes such as declining sales effectiveness, personal and professional risk for the Buyer and Seller, and culture-induced anxiety, and adds yet another layer to the management science of competitive selling, customer politics, and Power Bases. He highlights the importance of company culture and focuses on the Client-Centric Culture, the Looking Glass Culture, and the Confused Culture. The book grounds the reader with powerful messages, examples, and actionable steps to take forward within their own sales pursuits or to enable their organizations.

"This book is for sellers, sales managers, and company executives, ensuring everyone has the tools to achieve quality of life, and the ability to enjoy their work and have fun! *Selling in an Anxious World* clearly outlines how a gig culture has created anxiety and fear for both the seller and the buyer, where personal and professional risk is top of mind. It offers a clear strategy and steps for sellers and sales managers to focus on the customer once again. No longer are we focused on 'stuff' for the sake of managing optics of a shared calendar. Instead, we are empowered to bring value to the customer by listening and putting ourselves into our customers' shoes to reduce risk as it relates to their business. There is also a diagnostic tool for company executives, though I recommend everyone use it, to identify and characterize your company culture, so the gap is clearly seen and you can strategically work to ensure it is a culture your customers will value.

"Many companies grow through acquisition and each company has its own culture supported by its executives. Ultimately, it is influence and leadership, independent of authority that will determine the culture adopted by the combined organizations. Having a growth mindset vs. a fixed mindset allows for continuous process improvement and drives the breakthrough moments of being obsessed with customers' success. Sellers in a Client-Centric Culture are leaders focused on the business value, not the sale, and oversee the delivery of that value. They operate at a higher level of professionalism and integrity, knowing how to manage risk and politics while managing client-specific solutions and services, even if it is a large commodity deal.

"Cultural change takes leadership, political power, timing, and entrepreneurial ability, and with a quick review of Power Bases, Foxes (introduced in Power Base Selling and The Selling Fox), and Jackals, you will learn the qualities that are required to support effective cultural change. "Finding the 'right' Foxes and avoiding the Jackals is vital to protecting healthy cultures. Jackals are most recognized as they advance their interests at the expense of the company, the clients, and employees; they are masters at managing up.

"Selling is a combination of art and science. Jim Holden has masterfully included some poetry and quotes, along with stories from other domains—like mountaineering, dealing with adversaries in a law enforcement or counterterrorism role, and even cancer. These stories involve people confronting danger in emotionally charged situations and providing a way to characterize culture so we can better understand and manage it through these teachable moments.

"Holden provides sound recommendations for how to configure your important deal pursuit teams, including Team Mission Statement, to drive campaign success and avoid the Monkey Dance. You'll also be introduced to the new procurement advisor industry that has evolved to create significant business value for the buyer. It is a role that is complemented by the industry advisor on the sell side, whose goal is to produce increased business value for the client and competitive advantage for the seller. To assist companies in winning key opportunities with minimum business development cost, a campaign advisor on the sell side is continually testing all major client-facing activities throughout the campaign, building team expertise, and strengthening sales culture.

"Anyone who is on their selling game and is experiencing any fear or anxiety, constantly feeling the presence of risk, will now have insight into the causes and the solutions. With Holden's insights, we can navigate the ever-changing world. It is time to find the collective Foxes and direct caring to customers and employees, so the joy of selling is restored."

—Melinda Watson
former Regional VP & Head of NA
Global Sales Operations, SAP

"I would recommend this book to any seller in my industry, but perhaps not my competition. *Selling in an Anxious World* is both thought provoking and educational. I found myself rating my organization's culture, as well as the way I engage with my clients. In today's world of uncertainty, sellers need to be part of a culture that is outwardly focused on the buyers' business strategy, priorities, and success. Or, they need to be working to that end. This will be vital to growing revenue and profits, as well as market share through improved sales effectiveness. I encourage everyone to write down the strategies from this book and apply them to achieving their professional goals."

—Brian Oliversen
Select Account Manager,
Healthcare, Cisco

SELLING IN AN ANXIOUS WORLD

Driving Sales Success by Crossing the
Crevasse from Bad to Good Culture

JIM HOLDEN

Published by Holden LLC d/b/a Holden International, Chicago, Illinois.

ISBN: 978-1-7355632-0-6

Printed in the United States of America

CONTENTS

PART ONE
The Culture–Sales Relationship

PART TWO
A Deep Dive into Culture

PART THREE
Winning Important Deals

CHAPTER OVERVIEW

Foreword
By Patrick Nicolet

Introduction
What Sellers Are Seeing Today

PART ONE
The Culture–Sales Relationship

Chapter 1
The Culture–Sales Connection

Certain trends have resulted in a strong inward-company focus, the generic treatment of customers, and a sales culture that wrongly indicts sellers for nonperformance. This is a twenty-first century phenomenon that is creating environments of fear, defensiveness, and risk aversion at levels never seen before in the corporate world—and all at the expense of productivity and sales effectiveness.

Chapter 2
Assessing Your Culture

A diagnostic will help you differentiate good culture from bad culture, with the latter driving a strong inward company focus that is insensitive to clients and not winning business: the Looking Glass Culture.

Your executive leadership also has the ability to look at your company's culture in terms of what they want it to be and what it really is, which is the first step to building it up and providing customers with enhanced CX.

Chapter 3
Reshaping Culture

Culture is shaped and maintained by the collective control of powerful individuals where influence, not authority, rules. If you are a seller, you're in a unique position to drive sales and play a key role in shifting your company culture.

Chapter 4
Why Sales

Discover the five reasons why sellers are in the most significant position to effect culture change, while also driving revenue. Coupled with the right timing and entrepreneurial ability, building a support base of powerful individuals will place you in a strong leadership position to drive change, while securing important business.

PART TWO
A Deep Dive into Culture

Chapter 5
Culture and Politics

Important to shaping culture, you're introduced to the different types of Power Bases, Foxes, and Jackals, who (like Foxes) are powerful but dangerous to align with for so many reasons.

Chapter 6
Culture and Caring

You're introduced to what's really going on in colleges today and its impact on companies when hiring college graduates who can become liabilities and not assets. Charlie Kirk, Founder and Executive Director of Turning Point USA, will share his thoughts on this. You'll also see that what sits behind any culture is a caring for people, which is viewed in this chapter as being of finite amount within people and organizations. This is a new concept backed by observation and science.

Chapter 7
When Seeing Is Not Believing

When people become preoccupied with their company culture due to perceived career risk, they are not only in the culture, but of it. With a diminished ability to see what's really happening, the irrational becomes rational and sales decline.

Chapter 8
Putting a Face on Culture

You're introduced to the concept of personifying culture to better understand how it actually works, what drives it, what threatens it, and how it protects itself. You'll see how its strength and endurance is derived from the dynamic of potentiation, making it ready to destroy or purge anything that attempts to drive unwanted change.

PART THREE
Winning Important Deals

Chapter 9
The Pursuit Team

You'll be introduced to one of the most challenging situations a seller can face: the Monkey Dance. When a Looking Glass Culture asserts itself in the pursuit of an important deal, it puts the pursuit team lead in a lose-lose position. Either he sells in a manner consistent with culture and management directive, putting the deal at risk, or challenges the culture and directive, putting his job security at risk.

Chapter 10
Pursuit Team Mission

As part of an important sales pursuit this chapter presents the cornerstone to team success. Often overlooked, even in the largest and most important deal pursuits, is the team's mission statement. This is a living, breathing document that provides purpose, meaning, and direction to everything the team will do to win business.

Chapter 11
Buy-Side and Sell-Side Advisors

Here you'll see the mission and roles of procurement and industry advisors that support both sides of major deals with a primary focus on providing client value, which puts them at odds with a supplier Looking Glass Culture and the internal focus that it drives. Rj Smith, an industry advisor for the gaming and hospitality business, will share his thoughts on this.

Chapter 12
Sell-Side Support

In this last chapter, you were introduced to the campaign advisor who carries the mission of assisting a pursuit team in winning a specific piece of business, while building team expertise and strengthening sales culture to help win future important deals. In this chapter, you'll see seven critical thinking points that are highly material to winning important opportunities, particularly in bad supplier cultures.

Epilogue

Imagine that you're climbing a mountain that symbolizes the relationship with your customer. You've qualified the mountain in that conditions are good for the ascent from base camp, just as you would qualify an important opportunity. But unlike selling, if you make a mistake, you could die. This last part of the book deals with emotions that define and influence all of us when confronted with real challenge.

Quick Reference

Fast access to important concepts, ideas, and guidance.

Acknowledgements

FOREWORD

These are challenging, fast-changing times, but one thing remains constant: the importance of trust in human relationships. I first met Jim in December 2003, when I started leading sales for Capgemini Group. At the time, we were in post-crisis mode. I had to rebuild a sales engine to reach €10bn revenue per year on a sustainable basis. As a data-driven and performance-oriented leader, I always believe success in sales is 10 percent inspiration and 90 percent discipline and dedication.

I was searching for the best tools with which to equip our sales force. My attention was immediately caught by the rigor of Jim's methods. He loves mathematics and statistics; he never accepts a result that is not tested and proven, time and time again. Yet, even more importantly, Jim is passionate about sales—including selling to you.

We did a deal, developed a close collaboration, reached the objectives, and became friends. Ours is a relationship built on trust.

I was proud when Jim asked me to write this foreword. Knowing Jim as I have for the better part of two decades, I half expected to be commenting on another pioneering set of insights that he's discovered through successive rounds of data crunching. However, this time the insight is different. Rather than a quantitative analysis, Jim has created a qualitative assessment. He has turned his sagacity on a soft factor:

culture. He has considered the collection of behaviors that ultimately inhibit you from doing the sensical things to win.

While the focus this time is on softer skills, Jim retains his standard mathematical precision. Make no mistake, he has applied the same intellectual rigor to analyzing this less tangible aspect of sales that he has previously when qualifying opportunity, devising value statements, or assessing a powerbase in order to create the winning sales plan.

The timing of Jim's assessment of the sales process is apposite. The nature of workplaces is changing, perhaps irrevocably. Driven by a combination of technological development and socio-economic necessity, our workplaces and the relationships that take place within them—including business-to-business sales—have become increasingly digitized. In large enterprises, more and more business-development budget is going digital, from generating leads to supporting deals.

Technology, notably Artificial Intelligence (AI), is now deployed extensively to help sales teams identify targets, cultivate a detailed knowledge of existing clients, prioritize the parts of the portfolio that deliver the most benefits, build presentations, set quotas, develop commission schemes, and adjust terms and conditions. This AI-led digitization results in standard frameworks for sales executives that eliminate part of their creativity, but which also create freedom to focus on the most valuable element of the sales process: building trust.

In this context, Jim's focus on the softer side of sales is critical. While sales people now have more opportunity than ever before to cultivate strong relationships, there is also a global crisis in trust, reports Edelman's 2020 Trust Barometer (www.edelman.com/trustbarometer).

When decisions are prepared through data analysis, there is a key moment when an arbitrage must be made, when a commitment must be taken. You need to be able to trust people to sell to people, and you need to trust people in order to buy from them. Beyond the facts, trust will be the determining factor.

What emerges in this book is a complex picture of cultural concerns and political processes. Jim assesses how heightened uncertainty due to a conjunction of external and internal pressures means salespeople can fail to close a deal in the market, yet still keep face in the company, at least in the short term. Jim makes this political process tangible through personal experiences, helping the reader to translate the lessons they learn into their own world.

I went through this very process when reading this book for the first time—and it made me think that what Jim captures doesn't apply only to sales. The book shows how important it is that any modern business leader, regardless of their function, be able to build and engage in ecosystems. Some of your partners will deliver data, some will deliver spare parts, but you will have to engage in a range of different ecosystems.

In building an ecosystem, you engage resources to create a commitment to jointly deliver a product or service. An ecosystem needs a well-defined framework so that all participants have clear roles and responsibilities. Most critically, participants need to understand their part in the value of the product or service they create and the benefit they receive.

There could be a concern that ecosystem rules create constraints that constrict innovation. However, the ecosystem framework—similarly to the impact of AI in sales—actually frees up participants. Rather than worrying about responsibilities, participants can focus on delivering value and delighting customers, which builds trust between partners and on behalf of customers.

It's important to note that technology could potentially be deployed to automate elements of the exchange process in an ecosystem. However, automation is more usefully framed as an augmentation to human trust, rather than as a replacement, just as we must see AI as a way to augment human decision-making, rather than to obviate it.

Technology can automate repetitive tasks and create the freedom for us to use our time in more creative ways. What technology can't emulate is the rich relationship that emerges when two parties know each other and trust each other. In our digital age, which is characterized by constant change, the strength of trusted relationships brings welcome certainty.

Patrick Nicolet
Member of the Group
Executive Board and Group
CTO Capgemini

Introduction

What Sellers Are Seeing Today

"Today's anxiety is rooted in the progression of increased uncertainty driving increased perceived risk!"—Author

Sellers are living in an anxious and heightened risk-sensitive world. There has always been business risk in selling, but today, even before the current crisis, sales has become a risk-creating venture for both sellers and client individuals within their respective companies. In fact, fear associated with perceived risk has become so pronounced that in many sales situations the historical customer-buying considerations of price, performance, and delivery have been eclipsed by concerns of personal and professional risk. And this is happening on both the buying and selling sides of important opportunities, not only with customers, but with suppliers, which has some sellers rethinking whether they really want to be in sales.

A new type of company culture has emerged, which this book is going to unpack from the seller, executive, and client perspectives, while taking a hard look at how the new culture is driving down sales effectiveness and damaging sales careers—and what to do about it. This book is for a new generation of thinkers, and as such, you'll see how playing it safe to mitigate perceived risk is driving up anxiety within supplier and customer organizations.

This phenomenon became visible to our firm through the accumulation of data and the evolution of thought driven by careful observation over the last decade and interpreted by a lifetime of experience. Holden International saw the decline in sales results and connected it to supplier culture. We've worked with hundreds of clients over the years with a focus on the pursuit of very important deals that represented significant revenue, were highly visible within the supplier company, were highly political internally, and carried a high business development expense. It was these deals that first illuminated a culture problem. As we examined the phenomenon further we found that it was beginning to affect smaller—but still important—deals with sales anxiety and perceived risk aversion being common to both.

In this book we'll look at important deal pursuits as they shed light on this phenomenon, but make no mistake, selling is changing. We're going into a new era where sellers will continue to work somewhat remotely, avoiding wasteful time in commuting, while supported by strong IT infrastructure. This means rethinking work in a distributed environment for all of us. For sellers, it means engaging customers, partners, and others in an array of interlocking ecosystems that will initially be no easy task, given the need to build trust remotely amongst the growing levels of anxiety that exist within companies and their cultures today.

Let's say you're in pursuit of a key deal. It's the eleventh hour of the sales campaign and a client decision is about to be made. At the same time, the account has gone dark. The client is not calling you; not asking the kinds of questions that can be reasonably expected if they were looking at going forward. And if that isn't enough, your sales manager is insisting that you jump over your key contact's head and go to his boss to close the deal. You also know that when a sales situation is peaking, and you sense you have a problem, you usually have a disaster.

Managing the sales situation, even losing the deal, is one thing. But it's another to risk alienating your boss and potentially damage your career. That's fear-driven anxiety, manifested in the collision of internal and external conflict.

In another, but more personal example, suppose you have a credit problem with the bank and at the same time you have a sharp difference of opinion with your spouse on how it came about and how to solve it. Again, it's like being stuck between a rock and a hard place—that causes anxiety.

On the buy side of our sales example, heightened sensitivity and aversion to perceived risk (along with anxiety) are also ever present. Think about the implications if you acted on your manager's directive. Your key contact is already living in an environment of natural risk. When he makes a buying decision, or even a recommendation to his management, there's risk that it could be the wrong decision or could be perceived as the wrong decision by powerful individuals in management. While this has always been the case, personal and professional perceived risk have never been so high and closely tied together as in today's failure-sensitive corporate culture where activity is ironically taking precedent over results. That said, in our earlier example, what were your key contact's options? He could decide to go with you, not go with you, or make the decision not to decide and keep the evaluation in play, or simply kill it. *In today's world, do-nothing has become the major "competitor."*

Now add to that your jumping over your key contact's head and going to his boss. How will you be viewed? As a supplier and trusted partner committed to your key contact's success in making a good decision and implementing an effective approach to addressing their needs? Or as a supplier who is willing to compromise his client contact to close the deal? Jumping over his head is tantamount to saying that you don't have confidence in his ability to make the "right" decision to address his company's needs, which is also a negative reflection on his boss who assigned him the task—a task that your actions suggest he cannot handle.

In the best case you could contain yourself to a do-nothing decision and, in the worst case you could be immediately eliminated from the bid and possibly future business with the client. Yet, this is what many sellers are doing today: playing it safe within their companies to protect their standing in the company, as their careers are more important than any one deal. For many sellers, building an internal support base within their companies is more important than doing so with key accounts—even to the extent of doing so at the expense of building good client relationships. Yet, sellers are not at fault, as corporate culture in many companies today is forcing them to prioritize company and self over customer relationships and value.

We recently observed an example of client-risk intolerance when a firm's senior partner was heading up a major procurement. Several suppliers were asked to come in to discuss the requirements and present their thinking to a group of the firm's senior executives.

Each supplier brought in a team, asked good questions, and worked to demonstrate expertise and commitment in addressing the firm's requirements—except for one. That supplier showed up with just one guy. Maybe the supplier wasn't taking the opportunity seriously, or perhaps the company didn't have the people or resources to bring in a team. Whatever the reason, the partner in charge opened the meeting and confirmed that no one else from the supplier company was attending. He then closed the meeting and dismissed the supplier. The issue was not one of social protocol; it was about taking on perceived risk that didn't exist with the other suppliers. Demonstrating sharp and decisive leadership, the partner shut down the meeting and minimized the disruption to the schedules of the other executives. *This is risk management taking front and center priority during an important procurement, which for suppliers means fewer second chances.*

The deciding factor for clients today is who can do the job with the least amount of perceived risk. But at the same time, many sellers are doing just the opposite: increasing client risk, perhaps even unknowingly trampling on it. Today's supplier culture is also driving a strong and resilient inward focus for sellers and sales support personnel. Internal risk management has sellers focused on what they can control, being good team players, and what's good for their careers. Customers will come and go, but sellers need to live with and depend on people in their companies. Add to this the unending list of compliance demands that are put on sellers internally that is amplified by the rapid pace of change in the digital era and you have significantly less time for clients, that is, to really understand their businesses and build meaningful relationships with them, particularly in the new distributed environment. This increases customer perceived risk that, in turn, increases the supplier's risk of losing the business. As that happens, supplier management may put pressure on the seller to close the business, thus further alienating buyers. All of this contributes to a downward spiral of sales effectiveness.

The New Gig Culture

The world has changed. We now live in a gig culture and companies are not what they used to be. The term "gig" historically referred to musicians who would play a specific event or engagement. Initially, it suggested a short-term task performed by a contractor for a company. But today, the term goes well beyond that to reflect an environment driven by technology, automation, and culture, with the latter characterized by the need for personal independence and freedom of choice, individual self-interest, flexibility, and informality. We refer to it as the gig culture that exists as an overlay to the corporate world where company employees are experiencing job insecurity with staff augmentation in areas like IT outsourcing and business process outsourcing, and the increase in part-time and independent contract workers is becoming the norm.

"A new NPR/Marist poll finds that 1 in 5 jobs in America is held by a worker under contract. Within a decade, contractors and freelancers could make up half of the American workforce. Workers across all industries and at all professional levels will be touched by the movement toward independent work—one without the constraints, or benefits, of full-time employment"[1] But, all of this is not without its downside.

---

1 "Freelanced: The Rise of the Contract Workforce," npr.org, Jan. 22, 2018

What comes with this new and very dynamic global gig culture is a distinct lack of security, evidenced by:

- The erosion of traditional economic relationships between workers, businesses, and customers. In gig culture, people need to be able to move whenever a gig is present. There is no tomorrow. Any doubt and you're out. Decision-making must be fast to capture opportunities, lest they go to someone else. Full-time employees who once had security are now at constant risk of watching their job responsibilities move to independents. Outsource enough of them and a full-time job goes away; of course, so too do the years of experience, but that's a longer-term consideration that this culture does not appear to value. Yes, offloading responsibilities will extend the employee's capacity to perhaps focus on more important or interesting work, but it also reduces job security.

- Company growth strategies are centering on buy, sell, or merge inorganic growth with a heavy and understandable emphasis on scalability enabled through digital transformation and cost reduction. This has created a strong, resilient, and uncompromising inward focus of employees with sellers knowing very little about their clients, despite the abundant access to information on businesses and employees on the internet.

- Sellers have also become so activity oriented that they are driven to distraction and confuse being busy with making progress. It's easy to fill days, weeks, and months with meetings, travel, and other activities, and even easier to be ineffectively busy. It's more about managing the optics of shared calendars than real productivity. This heavy emphasis on doing *stuff* also reflects the high levels of employee distraction, overwork, impatience, and fear of career risk—all of which produce anxiety.

The gig culture is driving flexibility at the expense of personal security: less income confidence, rising consumer leverage, the disappearance of pensions, and more. Flexibility and volatility are producing a landscape of doubt and insecurity. And that has leaked to all four corners of company operations to produce institutional fear and perceived risk adversity that is affecting innovation and productivity within many firms today. Look around. Where is the innovation going? It's moving to the startups and SMEs (Small to Medium Enterprises) that have not been infected by the gig culture.

As an example, in financial services the real innovation today is not happening with the big guys but with the smaller independent hedge-funds where entrepreneurial spirit overrides gig culture. These companies and others may be small initially, but when their innovation creates new, productive, and welcome customer experiences their expansion can easily threaten legacy organizations on a global level.

In France in 2019, protestors disrupted the Christmas season once again. This time it was over pension reform with what *France 24 News* described as "a major overhaul of its pension scheme." The reform is to basically standardize the forty-two public and private pension systems, yet it can be considered one of the last bastions of security for some workers with a reported 54 percent of the population supporting the protests, in spite of all the inconvenience to people.

In Chicago, the teachers' union strike that put three hundred thousand students out of school ended in October 2019 with the union abandoning its community-interest demands in favor of a 16 percent increase in teacher pay over five years—another quest for security. How long unions everywhere can continue to fight gig culture remains to be seen.

That said, shifts in social values and reduced security are ever present in companies today. Digress from company norms that define its culture, hesitate to be a team player, and the "any doubt and you're out" feeling can kick in, creating fear and anxiety, which is now perceived by sellers, as mentioned earlier, to be sometimes worse than losing client business. This and a strong inward company focus, coupled with a scalable, but generic view of the world, has produced a decline in sales that has little to do with sales methodology, techniques, account planning, or anything related to seller ability.

Perhaps this sounds somewhat familiar. In our first book, *Power Base Selling, Secrets of an Ivy League Street Fighter* (1990), we wrote, "American companies, over a period of time, have become inwardly focused. It is no surprise that when high technology companies experienced a flattening in the marketplace in the mid-1980s they began to renew their commitment to customers." Well, it's time for companies to renew their commitment to customers once again.

The business quest for scalability has depersonalized and, in some cases, objectified clients to the point where sellers feel that the clients don't need to be understood or serviced in a client-specific way. This is seen with one-to-many marketing messages that sellers are expected to convey—essentially making sellers into marketers that call on accounts. They're becoming a new breed of inside and outside seller, operating as people did years ago in selling commodities when it was a game of numbers. Make enough calls, send out enough emails, and you too will be successful. It's the evolving one-to-many world of ineffective selling that is doomed in the developing distributed environment that we are living in today.

This book will take a clear and penetrating look at corporate culture based on solid observations where the pursuit of important opportunities has become the canary in the mine. These pursuits reflect what is good and bad about sales culture, directly impacting how sellers think and act, and very importantly, how customers respond to suppliers. These client responses illuminate what's *really* going on in corporate America and abroad. But we won't stop there.

The point of all this—now and as we emerge from the current crises—is to make a difference, in terms of suppliers providing more value to clients, driving more business, and rebuilding company culture to shift the focus back onto customers. This book is for sellers who not only want to be successful and build a career, but also desire quality of life and the ability to enjoy their work. It's about recognizing and navigating the incredible anxiety your buyers and decision-makers are feeling, while also recognizing your own anxiety that could have you drifting into an inward company focus to cope with that anxiety.

For many sellers, it's managing the fear of internal alienation for selling in an effective but countercultural way, in balance with managing the fear of losing the business if you follow internal cultural norms and expectations. Either can damage your career, as you conceptually bounce back and forth between internal and client expectations that conflict. All of this becomes very clear when pursuing important deals that often represent big or timely revenue for companies. These are deals that are very competitive, very internally political, very intense and visible, and in many cases, career making or breaking. But that doesn't mean winning such deals will secure a seller's future with the company. What's more important in today's gig culture is getting along internally; working in a manner that is consistent with company norms and what it values the most. When a seller operates countercul-turally and succeeds in winning business, that seller is seen as a threat to all others who are putting culture first and customers second. These are the people surrounding the seller who can limit resources and career advancement, along with taking other actions to either change seller behavior or purge them from the company, as any culture will destroy or force out what it can't assimilate.

This book is also for sales managers who see and recognize the decline in sales effectiveness today and want to understand and better manage how culture-induced anxiety is damaging productivity, innovation, and the customer centricity that is at the heart of profitable growth. In many companies, even before the current crises, pipeline volume was shrinking, velocity in the pipe was down, sales forecasting had become less accurate, win rates were decreasing, and while some large companies were market leaders, they were not growing as they should. *Sales managers can immediately help sellers drive business by reducing the noise that they have to deal with each and every day to free up time*—that is, time to research and better prepare for customer calls, proposals, and presentations. As a simple example, in today's company culture, five superficial sales calls per week are more valued than two with substance, as visible activity is prioritized over real results. The gig culture norm that says activity is safety, must change.

Finally, this book is for company executives who can also play key roles in directing company culture back to a client focus that is essential to growth. For those firms that want to seriously improve Customer Experience, this book will provide a diagnostic tool to characterize and define your company culture. *You will see the culture that the executive team believes exists and be able to compare it to the actual culture that sellers know to be true, as they directly deal with its impact on sales that makes it very visible to them.* Seeing the gap between the two is strategically invaluable. Company executives may see and live in one culture, but not know where it leaves off and another culture begins—one that is different and damaging at the operations and mid-management levels.

What this will also do is drive long-term customer satisfaction, which directly impacts future business. And again, the culprit standing in the way of progress right now is not sellers, sales managers, or company executives, per se, but culture. Deloitte's *Global Human Capital Trends* report covering more than seven thousand executives in 130 countries stated that only 28 percent of respondents report that they understand their organization's culture well, and only 12 percent believe they have the "right culture."[2] Unfortunately, the solution in many companies is to change out the salespeople. It's simply easier to blame sellers than to indict the culture and the powerful people who are part of it. This is an approach that only makes the problem worse by reducing tenure and expecting new sellers to somehow perform differently—an approach that speaks to the definition of insanity, but in the professional world.

---

2 www2.deloitte.com/content/dam/Deloitte/global/Documents/HumanCapital/ gx-dup-global-human-capital-trends-2016.pdf

What all this means is that something must change, and the best way to drive that change is from both a bottom-up *and* top-down approach. Executive management in conjunction with sellers who have one foot in their companies and one foot in client organizations can shift culture for everyone's benefit. All of this did not happen by design, but as an unintended consequence of new thinking in society and in companies that, along with other factors, are driving the company growth strategy mentioned earlier. This is an economy and culture that has evolved over many years with shifting values and slow GDP growth. That said, things can change. And change is what this new book is all about.

We all see the decline in sales effectiveness. Arthur Schopenhauer, the German philosopher, said, "The task is not to see what has not yet been seen, but to think what no one has thought about that which everyone sees." Our goal in writing this book is to show you how to think differently about culture, how to create a new sales effectiveness narrative that looks at corporate culture, and how to drive higher levels of professional and personal success. At the same time, you can be building your own personal sales philosophy, as no real good can happen *through* you until it first happens *to* you.

This book also provides you with brief chapter descriptions in the Chapter Overview to enable you to quickly get to what is important to you. In addition, the Quick Reference, at the end of the book, replaces old-style word indexing to make key insights in the book also available for a fast read, getting straight to specific concepts, ideas, and guidance that are relevant to you and your work.

SELLING IN AN ANXIOUS WORLD

In gig culture where the vibrancy of youth and the wisdom of experience come together, this book offers business redefined in an effort to merge creativity and intellect:

This is business redefined,
To give what can't be bought.
It's art and logic combined,
To feel the power of thought.
—Author

PART ONE

The Culture–Sales Relationship

1

The Culture–Sales Connection

"The most important thing is to be customer obsessed, figure out how to absolutely delight them."—Jeff Bezos, CEO of Amazon

A new phenomenon has emerged in corporate America. It began with a slow economy and shifting values that morphed into the gig culture of today. This combined with an ever-growing and popular company-growth strategy, is casting an ever-darkening shadow upon sales. In the pursuit to achieve steady, predictable, and profitable growth, an unintended consequence is developing that will ironically damage the very growth that brought it to life. Companies, often without realizing it, are subjugating customers to an unprecedented level of internal focus that is crippling sales. Evidenced by the pursuit of large important deals where sales campaigns are highly visible, intensely political, and fiercely competitive, customers are ranking last. In this age of hyper-connectivity and abundant information, sellers have never known less about their customers' business, vision, direction, and priorities. Sellers have never been busier—often driven to distraction—and never been less concerned about the welfare and success of their clients. This is a phenomenon of company culture that has turned dark and is driving sales effectiveness into the ground across all areas of sales and marketing from retail to commercial to government procurements.

Customer Experience (CX) is a watchword in today's retail world of business-to-consumer (B2C) marketing, and yet according to Qualtrics, "There is a massive gap between the experiences companies offer and the experiences a new generation of consumers demand. When polled, 80% of CEOs believe they are delivering a superior experience, but only 8% of customers agree."[1] And this is happening even though the stock performance of CX leaders clearly outperforms that of CX lagging companies, according to industry analyst group Forester.[2] And the picture is no different in the business-to-business (B2B) space.

B2B company CEOs are under tremendous pressure quarter to quarter to drive predictable and profitable growth. This has led many CEOs to adopt what appears to be the prevailing approach to driving revenue. It's a strategy that operates in a machine-like manner, combining the elements of acquisition/divestiture/merger and scalability—all enabled by digital transformation and cost reduction. Pure R&D to drive innovation continues to be important but is often considered too slow in a gig culture. This is a sophisticated growth strategy that is machine-like in its systematic approach to driving steady revenue growth—one that can be nicely packaged, communicated, understood, and operationalized throughout a company, which is essential to support the integration of acquired companies into the organization. People relate to it and therefore how to apply it directly or indirectly

---

1   www.qualtrics.com/blog/ai-experience-economy
2   www.forrester.com/hub/analysts.xhtml

within their departments, which is good, but at the same time it tends to drive a strong inward focus. Understandably, this has allowed the growth strategy to expand within companies to areas like marketing and sales where technology is no stranger and where scalability has become all important. But is this strategy responsive to customers?

As the growth strategy gets close to the actual sources of revenue it begins to cause problems. And the closest physical point to revenue is sales, which is being turned inward, away from customers, and consumed by the force of machine-like gravity into marketing. Don't get me wrong; strong alignment between marketing and sales is essential, but this goes beyond alignment. The growth strategy has taken the focus off of customers, almost "dehumanizing" them, and turning a blind eye to understanding who they really are and what they require. While customers expect to see solution approaches and business value that are specific to their needs, they instead get one-to-many messaging that is often not specific, even to their industry.

In that sense, the word "solution" is a misnomer, as the real focus is on products and services and not the problems they solve for customers. Maybe that's okay if you're in retail or selling commodities or perhaps pharmaceuticals where sellers are reciting scripted generic messages along with providing samples. But if you're in the B2B solutions business, sellers cannot be the personification of nondescript one-to-many marketing messages. If they are, they essentially become marketers where there's no need to know and understand or be close to the customer. This creates a multitude of sales issues not the least of which is dealing with competition.

From a competitive point of view, differentiation comes from within the offering: its capabilities and how they are applied; and from how sellers sell: positioning value, building a politically strong support base, and formulating a solid compete strategy. If sellers don't know the customer, they can't determine how competitive differences in their products are relevant to the customer. They also won't know the political landscape within the account, in terms of who to sell to in order to build sales momentum and support. And if all this is the case, do you really need a sales force? Wouldn't a direct marketing team doing inside sales with limited account visits do just as well?

If you know B2B selling, you will likely say no. Yet, the unintended consequence of the prevailing growth strategy in our gig culture is effectively making sellers into marketers. And that is something that's leading to lost deals, reduced pipeline volume, less accurate and timely sales forecasting, and worse yet, the indictment of sellers, suggesting that *they* are the problem. This perceived sales incompetence has become very visible in companies where we see increased turnover and low tenure in the sales force. In some cases, the tenure equals the ramp-up time for new sellers, creating a sales organization that is dramatically underpowered. Sellers are being replaced since company executives view them to be the problem, not recognizing the real culprit. Yet for the most part, sellers are simply scapegoats. It's company culture that really sits behind the decline or lack of expected growth in sales.

Driving this decline in sales effectiveness is first and foremost a sales-averse culture that rewards itself with a strong inward focus.

A recent *Wall Street Journal* article, "Consulting Firms Make Inroads into the Business of Ad Agencies," stated: "A large international consulting firm's team arrived at Puma's Boston office wearing suits and Puma shoes and proceeded to give a long presentation about 'digital transformation,' Mr. Hassenstein says. 'The presentation looked very similar to one the consulting firm had given previously to another business unit within Puma,' he adds. *'There were 80 slides full of prophecies and bubbles,'* Mr. Hassenstein says. 'I was confused, and it was a very deterring experience.'"[3]

The question that CEOs, whose companies are providing B2B solutions, should be asking to their heads of sales today is, "Are we effectively calling on customers? And, how much time are we spending to really understand our customers' businesses?" Attendance counts. Not just showing up, which is a good start, but also being there mentally with good preparation, questions, and dialog that are tied to the customer's business. Being there emotionally and showing care and real interest in contributing to the client's business should be the definite subtext to any customer meeting. Unfortunately, this is not often the case today, as it is not something valued in gig culture. Sales performance has been informally redefined, and as a result it is degrading at a rapid pace across large companies, major industries, and developed countries. This is not due to a lack of sales ability, process, or techniques, but because the sales environment has shifted in the wrong direction.

Not only are sellers not "customer obsessed," as Jeff Bezos advises, they are not even customer aware. They're simply not focused on clients or understanding their business and what drives it. In an age

---

3   www.wsj.com/articles/consulting-firms-make-inroads-into-the-business-of-ad-agencies-11560823320

of nearly instantaneous access to copious amounts of information, sellers have never had less insight into their customer base. *With hyperconnectivity, it's easy to communicate and easier to communicate ineffectively due to distraction and lack of time.*

"Beware the barrenness of a busy life," said Socrates. It's better to do two things well than ten things half baked. For example, if each seller is making only two effective customer calls per week and you have two hundred sellers, that's pushing twenty thousand very effective calls per year. The aggregated value becomes significant and that's only two solid customer calls per week. Activity cannot be allowed to supersede quality, whether it be phone calls or customer visits. In the case of the latter, sellers have never had less face-to-face client selling time than in today's digital world. With short attention spans, sellers are as much driven by distraction as they are results. Activity has become confused with progress. Worse yet, internally focused activities that are insensitive to client needs create negative progress, expressed in lost deals. And yet ironically, these sales behaviors are being supported by company management, and being perpetuated, as they infect big deals and small.

The canary in the mine is the very large deal that is highly visible, highly political, highly competitive, highly significant to revenue and margin growth, highly expensive to pursue, and highly important to large clients. This is where the truth lies and where this book focuses—on resolving the growing conflict between a sales-averse company culture and winning important deals. It's about solving the cultural preoccupation problem to sell more, provide more value to clients, and advance seller careers, not damage them.

The Lead-up to Cultural Decline

"You are a product of your environment. So, choose the environment that will best develop you toward your objective. Analyze your life in terms of its environment. Are the things around you helping you toward success—or are they holding you back?"—W. Clement Stone.

Cultures change and people change. Knowing who you really are, as a person, is knowing how the culture you live in has evolved. It's about the history of your culture shaping your identity.

Not long ago, sales process was a new concept. Sellers recognized that if you skipped steps in the selling process you were likely to have to make them up later in the sales cycle when it was much more difficult. At the same time, company management recognized that tracking and managing sales process was key to forecasting sales, scheduling resources, and meeting delivery requirements. This led to pipeline management and Customer Relationship Management (CRM) that captured customer information and sales activities. But all of this was product centric, as everything was viewed through the lens of product.

Sellers focused almost exclusively on product features, benefits, price, and delivery. And that made sense to a lot of people. After all, the product provided something tangible, and often customers needed to be educated on what it could and could not do. Before the gig culture, the sales role itself was essentially one of relationship-building, educating customers, product-positioning, and closing. But it was also one that reflected a very comfortable kind of thinking. As sellers peered through the product lens, if everything tended to look like a nail it was nice to be in the hammer business.

Over time, the internet made information far more accessible with some suppliers being down selected by customers without ever being contacted. Conversely, customers expected sellers to know their business by doing their homework before entering accounts. Sales cycles took a major shift in that regard and the sales process became more sophisticated to include qualifying opportunities. Sellers could objectively determine if a deal was real and could be won. Prior to that point, the reality was that any opportunity that was warm, breathing, and had a pulse was qualified. No sales manager would allow a seller to qualify anything out without a struggle, as every deal was considered important. Quantified evidence that an opportunity shouldn't be pursued was helpful, but it was still not easy for a seller to avoid pursuing deals that could never be won. Such opportunities might have been bad business, in terms of the supplier not being able to really do the job for the customer, or because of the risk of not getting paid due to the customer's financial condition, or perhaps due to strong evidence that suggested an inability to defeat a well-entrenched competitor. Whatever the reason, sales process didn't stop there. Building a sales campaign, creating value-centered proposals, conducting effective presentations, dealing with customer objections, defeating competitors with strategy that anticipated their actions, and closing the business came into focus for a lot of sellers who viewed selling as a true profession. But not all did, and as the very early signs of the gig culture began to develop, seller behavior began to change.

With formalized sales process came visibility. And with visibility came individual sales accountability not just for results, but for how those results were achieved, in terms of sales activity and internal cultural alignment. Sellers were now tracked by pipeline management reports and their progress monitored throughout sales cycles. CRM reports gave managers the ability to zero-in on anything they felt sellers weren't doing right, which exposed salespeople to time consuming justification discussions at the least and criticism that could be career damaging at the worst. That said, sellers adjusted their behavior, limiting their exposure and risk by putting as little information into CRM systems as possible. When companies made CRM reporting mandatory to getting paid, sellers simply complied by entering data a day or two before closing deals and staying silent on everything else. Win rates looked great, CRM data was entered, and all were happy—except sales managers, as forecast accuracy suffered, but it was a small price to pay for sales excellence evidenced by reported win results.

The point here is that sellers adapt to whatever they feel is important and avoid whatever they feel is not important—a behavior that has not changed over time. If cultural norms are most important, they will dominate all else, even sales effectiveness.

The Prophecies and Bubbles Culture Shift

Filling out call reports and CRM data sheets, securing management approvals, briefing internal stakeholders, and more became part of the job for sellers, but it was at the expense of face-to-face selling time—a precious commodity that could not be recaptured. And so, a cultural shift began to take place. Slowly and surely, seller focus began to turn inward at the expense of account coverage. Technological innovation that discovered how to communicate in the absence of special and temporal coincidence had reached a new level, as sellers had to deal with a continuous and growing stream of daily emails, numerous lunch-and-learns, and webinars. Hyperconnectivity was born and what came with it was a strong emerging culture of inward focus. Internal compliance with the company growth strategy expanded and grew, intensifying the cultural shift within companies. Not surprisingly sellers adapted to their environment by putting more emphasis on internal compliance than on sales effectiveness and customer satisfaction. Working to the norms of company culture was now out of balance with understanding and meeting the needs of customers to the point where sales losses could be justified when doing the "right" things internally. Back to our *Wall Street Journal* example:

> Consulting firms are seeing big revenue increases as a result of moving into marketing and advertising, but some say there are still culture clashes. . . . And firms that have grown quickly, sometimes as a result of acquiring creative shops, are struggling to bring together contrasting cultures of advertising and consulting. They are not always in tune with advertisers' needs.

The sales culture had shifted and so had sales behaviors. But like the adage of boiling a frog, it had happened slowly enough not to be super visible to company management, particularly given that some senior executives didn't want to acknowledge it in the first place. They saw the decline in sales effectiveness but attributed it to bad sales, which meant bad sellers. This led to higher turnover in sales organizations that simply exacerbated the problem. But for sellers, denial was not an option.

The truest assessment of company culture is through the eyes of the sellers in the field, as they have direct access to both their own companies and their customers' organizations. They see it and live it all. And where they see culture most clearly is in the pursuit of important opportunities, often within major accounts. It's these often-larger deals that propel the development of any account, and it is these opportunities that most illuminate the supplier's culture. The good and the bad of any culture is exposed in these instances, and when that culture works against important sales campaigns, it costs revenue, growth, margin, and customer satisfaction. Moreover, it does so in such a way that it causes sales effectiveness problems to grow and grow, reinforcing bad culture in a way that eclipses the importance of having the right selling process or the right account planning methodology. While important, these skills and practice-based approaches to selling will not succeed if they are held down by a bad sales culture that drives an inward focus at the expense of customer-centricity. The problem created by gig culture and machine-like growth strategy has produced unintended consequences, in terms of lost deals of all sizes.

Summary of Chapter 1

In this chapter, we identified factors that have contributed to bad culture: the gig economy and its evolution to the now gig culture and its shifting values, coupled with the buy, sell, or merge company-growth strategy that is dependent on mass scalability and powered by digital transformation and cost reduction. These trends have resulted in a strong inward company focus, the generic treatment of customers, and a sales culture that wrongly indicts sellers for nonperformance. This is a twenty-first century phenomenon that is creating environments of fear, defensiveness, and risk aversion at levels never seen before in the corporate world—and all at the expense of productivity and sales effectiveness.

But what's being done about it now that the pursuit of important deals has illuminated the problem?

Repairing a bad culture, no matter what its cause, is no easy task, but it begins with understanding what culture actually is and is not, which we'll address in the next chapter.

2

Assessing Your Culture

"There are people in the world who have the power to change our values." —John Mayer

Psychologists define culture in terms of "specific traditions, morals, concepts, insights, art, or dialect of a commune or society characterized by the symptomatic outlooks and actions of a specific group within society, like a social hierarchy class, or age."[1] Scientists view it as "sets of unwritten rules for interacting with one another. In science, these rules of good behavior are fairly general but are essential to maintaining the quality of scientific evidence and ideas."[2] Business leaders explain it as an "organization's expectations, experiences, philosophy, as well as the values that guide member behavior, and is expressed in member self-image, inner workings, interactions with the outside world, and future expectations. Culture is based on shared attitudes, beliefs, customs, and written and unwritten rules that have been developed over time and are considered valid" (*The Business Dictionary*). The Bible speaks about culture by saying, "Do not be

1   www.psychologydictionary.org
2   www.undsci.berkeley.edu

conformed to this world, but be transformed by the renewal of your mind, that by testing you may discern what is the will of God, what is good and acceptable and perfect" (Romans 12:2).

Psychologists, scientists, and business leaders all take a somewhat conceptual approach to defining culture, and for good reason: culture is situationally defined, specific to each company. Understandably, these definitions are broad, but they all insist that culture basically defines how things get done within an organization. The Bible, however, takes a different approach. It doesn't seek to define culture, as in the above passage, but rather to focus on the acceptability of culture. *It acknowledges that people need to be in the world, but at the same time, don't need to be controlled by the world.* Independent of your religious views, this useful piece of instruction indicates that one should not simply conform to a culture. Instead, question it, push back, test it, and, in the process, renew your mind.

This is exactly the challenge that needs to be faced by every company competing in the B2B market space today that is not customer obsessed. So, what are we actually pushing back on? Culture can be viewed as a living, breathing force within a company. Why? In short, because it has the ability to exert influence over the behavior of people within the culture. In that sense, cultural inhabitants are actually not totally independent individuals but people operating under the influence of a culture. It starts at 8:30 or so in the morning when we arrive at work and ends at 5 or 6 p.m. when we leave. Arriving home is not the worker but the individual, the person whose behavior is his own, assuming that work did not follow him home. For what follows with work is the work culture. But it is this behavior, independent of work, that defines the individual, hopefully everywhere, but more often just outside of work. Inside work, we all tend to map into the culture to get things done and to some extent be viewed favorably by others as a team player.

We also see this cultural influence on people in social settings where the motivation is not to get things done but to be accepted within a social group. That's human nature. It's not a bad thing necessarily, unless the culture of the social circle influences or changes a person in a way that is counter to who that person really is or wants to be in life. It may also come into conflict with who the employer wants the individual to be as a representative of the company. When people map into a particular culture, it changes them over time. And the more defined and structured the culture, the faster this will occur.

Some time ago, when formally structured cultures were more prevalent, I worked with a leading computer company that not only imposed its culture on employees, but also on suppliers. Acceptable behaviors were identified by policy, including a dress code that was enforced to project a common and professional image. The employees of this company were good people with good intentions, dedicated to the firm. As a result of the strong culture, their self-identity and self-worth reflected their work, the value they provided to the company, and the excitement of working for a respected and well-known industry leader. However, when the time came to retire and leave the work culture, they essentially discovered a person empty and devoid of purpose and meaning in life. In my view, despair led to depression, taking a heavy toll on their health, as the average retiree was dead in thirteen months.

Think of it as suddenly not knowing who you are—not because of a disease like Alzheimer's but because you had mapped into a strong and formally structured culture for so long that you basically lost sight of who you were in life outside of work. Today, gig culture has changed all of that as we see company cultures that are different, but just as strong, and which are driving the decline in sales effectiveness. Unlike the past, these cultures are not defined and structured by visible authority and policy, but by the informal invisible exertion of influence on people. Company politics, as its own self-actualizing force that can make or break careers, has never been stronger or more assertive as it is in companies today.

This brings us to why it is so incredibly difficult to change and evolve culture, as the people who are *in* the culture *become* the culture. How do you solve a problem from within when you have become part of the problem? The answer is that you don't; and that's the wisdom of the Bible that references an external force that can be leveraged to create change. God becomes a powerful third party to help people recognize the difference between being part of the world and being in the world, which is analogous to seeing the difference between the you at work and the you at home, or the difference between how you see your sales culture within your company and how your clients see your sales culture based upon how they are treated.

Change, and knowing who you really are, begins with this recognition. It's only then that you can set out to be the real you in any environment, whether it's at work, at home with family, at church, out with friends, or during those quiet moments of reflection when you're alone and being introspective. It's knowing when not to compromise based upon the recognition that the best thing you have going for you is the real you. This means knowing the you that you're meant to be in life—the autonomous you; knowing what you value and how to defend it in any environment.

These same questions apply to your company. What should the sales culture really be and how is that different from what it is today? This book is not about playing God but about assisting you to look at your culture through the eyes of your customers who are credible third-parties. The goal is not only to drive your own personal sales success as a seller, or your company's sales if you are a sales manager or executive, but to change the culture within your sales organization, to bring fun back into the work, to build better customer relationships through value and the integrity of your company, to do the job as it was meant to be done.

We know that the sales cultures within many companies today, both domestically and internationally, are sick and are driving a decline in sales or limiting growth with significant opportunity cost. We see it over and over again by physical observation and through our participation in advising clients on large-deal pursuits. As an objective third party with strong sales development experience, we also know that this sickness is infecting sellers all around the world. And, as that happens, more and more sellers become part of the problem, reinforcing a bad culture in a way that self-aggravates to the negative.

As the story goes, take a cage of ten monkeys and put a banana at the top of a rock formation within the cage, and every time a monkey climbs the rocks, spray all of them with a water hose. Do this many times and no monkey will attempt the climb. Then, remove one monkey and put a new one into the cage. What happens when he attempts to climb up and get the banana? The others stop him, as they don't want to be sprayed by the water hose. This is culture taking on a life of its own, growing in strength, and protecting itself, as any culture will tend to destroy or purge itself of whatever it can't assimilate. The Romans 12:2 Bible verse tells us to "test" ourselves against "what is good and acceptable and perfect," by God. As you look at what sales culture should be, test it against what customers feel a supplier's sales behavior should be, in order to be good and acceptable. This brings the voice of the customer into the picture with clarity and thoughtfulness to make clear what is a good vs. a bad sales culture.

A bad sales culture promotes a strong inward focus at the direct expense of customer face-to-face time and customer insight that is critical to addressing their needs and producing strong customer satisfaction. These cultures are incessantly focused on themselves, sacrificing existing and new customer relationships by feeding on an array of internal demands and compliance requirements. In these organizations, change is often good for its own sake; the next new thing is good, new technology-enabled process is good, and when one person leaves a position, existing practices and processes often leave with that individual. Constant change creates a false sense of progress, institutionalizing a strong inward focus that diminishes the need to meet with prospective customers, as strange as that might sound. Combine this with ever-expanding company portfolios of differentiated products and services with numerous internal stakeholders, gate keepers, and the like, and you have an exponentially increasing inward focus that is most visible when an organization needs to pull together to pursue and win large and important opportunities.

Winning these opportunities is incredibly important. Large revenue potential combined with the high business development expense to pursue such deals makes them a high-risk, high-reward venture. As such, these pursuits receive a lot of attention and resources in order to effectively map into the customer's requirements in a way that is differentiated from the competition. Such large-deal pursuits become the epicenter for all kinds of support and executive involvement, which means, internally, they are highly visible and extremely political. They also require flexibility in terms of the sales campaign, building and modifying customer solutions, delivery of solutions, and sometimes requiring changes in business practices. It is this required customer-centric flexibility that finds itself at odds with a bad sales culture, which is ironic in a gig culture that favors flexibility.

What Culture Are You Living In?

So now, you be the test of what is good and acceptable in your sales culture by being sales specific to illuminate how your sales culture has a positive or negative effect on win rates for important deal pursuits. If you're a seller or sales manager, review each of the following questions, and answer them, YES or NO, based upon what you have experienced in your company's sales culture. Pick the most significant deal that you are familiar with and use that as your baseline for a sales culture assessment. If you're a corporate executive, answer the questions based upon your perception of what's happening at the operational and field levels or what you believe the culture should be as part of your vision for the business:

1. Would you say that the pursuit team is larger than necessary, involving people who don't play a direct role in the sales campaign, as there may be individuals who provide support or input to the team but don't actually need to be involved in all team activities, as in being part of the core team that is principally responsible for winning the business? Yes or No?

2. Does the pursuit team demonstrate leadership by committee vs. the pursuit manager having command and control over the pursuit, in terms of campaign strategy that works to a theme of customer business value that is differentiated from competition, as well as in terms of managing day-to-day operational sales activities? Yes or No?

3. Is it acceptable in your sales culture for executives to pulse into a sales campaign and redirect it in a manner that is contrary to the pursuit manager's wishes or is customer contraindicated for whatever reason? Yes or No?

4. Is the pursuit team ever pressured to close a deal within a short period of time or within the quarter, for example, when the team knows that the customer's priorities and/or time-lines don't support a buying decision at that point in time? Yes or No?

5. Is the pursuit team somewhat disconnected from the customer or less sensitive to the customer or less knowledgeable about the customer and their business than should be the case, which

can often occur when a team is consumed with busy work, such as managing email, internal relationships, resources, and other compliance policies and requests? Yes or No?

6. Does the pursuit team appear to be more concerned with pleasing, responding to, or spending time with people internally rather than with the customer, as evidenced by the amount of customer face-to-face time, customer research, or competition research? Yes or No?

7. Is there any lack of understanding or confusion about the customer's business, including its vision, direction, and priorities and how your company's solutions will advance that direction with a specific customer executive priority identified? Yes or No?

8. Is there an attitude that the customer should align itself or adapt itself to your solution and implementation or alter its policies and procedures rather than your company demonstrating flexibility to accommodate the customer's business, and what's important to the customer in how the solution gets implemented? Yes or No?

9. Is the solution value to the customer operationally and cost-reduction focused and not directly or indirectly tied to advancing a customer corporate executive priority, such as increasing revenues and/or margin, accelerating revenue, decreasing business risk for the customer, or something else that is mission critical to the customer? Yes or No?

10. Are your company's sales support materials or proposals and presentations generic in nature, perhaps to project consistent

market messaging, but also independent of specific customer needs? Yes or No?

11. Are pursuit team members building relationships with mostly operational-level customer individuals, as opposed to customer contacts who are known to have exerted strong influence, perhaps working in exception to policy or rarely being surprised by company events or demonstrating the ability to influence decisions across departmental lines, which are outside the person's area of authority? Yes or No?

12. Does the pursuit team seem to take a single-thread, or one-to-one vs. one-to-many, approach to account coverage, which is largely centered on one or just a few customer individuals, as opposed to calling on an array of customer stakeholders who consist of everyone that could be positively or negatively impacted by the effectiveness and success of your solution? Yes or No?

Scoring and Significance

Holden International sees sales culture firsthand, as an innovator in the sales development business, living in the world of sales, and having more than seven hundred clients over four decades. A part of our business centers on a critical-deal consulting practice that provides clients with direct support in the pursuit of important opportunities involving all aspects of sales campaign planning, preparation, and execution. Insights from these activities and the live deals we address during globally run sales development workshops have enabled us to observe firsthand the cultural phenomenon and inward focus that is damaging sales campaigns across industries and regions. The scoring below is based upon these observations and interventions with major companies:

Client-Centric Culture—If you scored 0 to 2 YES responses, you've identified that you have a predominately outward-focused sales culture that puts the customer first, as evidenced by the company's actions. This culture is a manageable asset to winning deals, as long as any culturally induced sales problems are quickly recognized and addressed. These sales cultures are good places to work and contribute to the following business outcomes:

- Strong P/L, based upon sales revenue and cost of sale,
- High customer satisfaction,
- Higher than industry average win rates,
- Shorter sales cycle times,
- Reliable sales predictability and forecasting,
- Low seller turnover that attracts high sales performers.

Here, the sales force is bright and visible, shining a light on sales opportunities and company growth. This is a CX Leader company.

Looking Glass Culture—If your review of these questions scored 6 or more YES responses, you've identified a predominately inward-focused sales culture that puts your company first, subjugating the customer to your company's needs. Like looking in a mirror, this culture's focus is on itself, even at the expense of winning the largest and most important deal pursuits, which can make it a bad place to work. It's a customer reflection that is either right side up or down, with the latter characterized by the following business outcomes:

- An inability of the pursuit team to compete with the sales culture, in terms of building and implementing an effective sales campaign,
- Unacceptable P/L, based upon sales revenue and cost of sale,
- Lower than industry customer-satisfaction and win rates, to the point of losing deals to other suppliers that are a lot less proven or capable,
- High seller turnover with low seller experience levels and few high sales performers
- Low pipeline volume and velocity,
- Low sales forecast accuracy, particularly relative to new account opportunities.

Here, the sales force has faded away, a shadow of its former self. This is a CX laggard company that likely is experiencing significant opportunity cost in lost revenues.

Confused Culture—If you scored 3 to 5 YES responses, you've identified a sales culture that is a mix of Client-Centric Culture and Looking Glass Culture, a kind of emulsion, a combining of oil and water in a way that confuses its inhabitants. And that confusion can make it an ugly place to work. While it doesn't help sales campaigns, it can definitely damage them. Confused cultures contribute to the following business outcomes, relative to Client-Centric Cultures:

- Marginal P/L, based upon sales revenue and cost of sale,
- Lower than industry customer-satisfaction and win rates,
- Higher than industry average seller turnover,
- Increased business development costs,

- Lower pipeline volume and velocity,
- Reduced sales forecast accuracy.

Here, the sales force is fading a little more each day. This is a CX laggard company with some customers and a CX leader with others, all based upon individual seller and sales manager strength. In addition, the company is likely experiencing some level of opportunity cost in lost revenues.

Summary of Chapter 2

In this chapter, we've defined culture and established the power it has over people. Nevertheless, while you may have to be *in* it, you don't need to be *of* it. Knowing yourself is key to maintaining the autonomous you and not becoming totally a product of your environment. Similarly, knowing your company culture—as clients see it—is also key. It's knowing what you value, your company values, and what your customers value, and how they all play together. To help with this, you now have a diagnostic to differentiate good from bad culture with the latter driving a strong inward company focus that is insensitive to clients and not winning business. Your executive leadership also has the ability to look at your company's culture in terms of what they want it to be and what it really is, which is the first step to building it up and providing customers with enhanced CX.

In our next chapter, we will introduce the concept of the influential collective who can enhance and change culture from within a company with sales taking the lead. For you who live in a Client-Centric Culture, this means the opportunity to strengthen and defend your culture while accelerating your sales success and building your leadership skills. For you who are living in a Looking Glass or Confused Culture, this means the opportunity to initiate cultural change while operating counterculturally to better serve your clients and drive sales success. In both cases, you will build significant insight in how to assess the culture of other companies, whether they are clients or companies that you might want to join at some point.

3

Reshaping Culture

"But what binds us together, though, is not our success;

it's the success that our customers achieve . . ."

—*Satya Nadella, CEO of Microsoft*

Business academics will tell you that company executives can change culture based upon their position and authority. It's true that company founders set the acceptable mindset and behaviors within a startup—often based upon their personal values—and that company executives have the power to initiate and support cultural change. *But that said, all organizations will eventually adopt a type of collective control of their culture, independent of authority and very much driven by influence.*

This recognizes that influence and authority are not synonymous. You can have high-level executives that have significant authority but little influence in certain areas of the business. Conversely, lower-level people with less authority can have influence greater than their position or rank. This gives them the ability to shape decisions across departmental lines, work in exception of policy, situationally influence culture, and more. Certainly, there are high-level individuals with both authority and influence, just as there are people with little authority and little influence, but it's the influential collective of cultural inhabitants that create, strengthen, and change a culture. A strong and new charismatic leader can act as a catalyst to change, but the actual change itself will only occur when a critical mass of the right influential individuals support the change, evidenced by the decisions and actions that drive new thinking, mindsets, and behaviors. But who are these people that make up the influential collective?

Throughout a company, the influential collective is generally made up of high performers who also have high organizational influence. To categorize this group, we first need to look at the distribution of influence within company functions, departments, and levels from operations to management to the executive suite. However, if you're reading this book and professionally living in a Looking Glass Culture, you and the cultural inhabitants around you will likely find what we're about to cover as somewhat counterintuitive or, simply stated, just plain strange.

That's because Looking Glass Cultures often steer and drive sellers to a single-thread sales approach in pursuing opportunities. This happens because of a culturally inward focus on product that's strong enough to limit the customer focus to operations-type individuals. Limiting the type and number of client individuals called on, limits the feedback and client-reflected visibility into your own culture, thus making it more difficult for you to see and understand what's actually happening in your own culture.

Not long ago, we did extensive work with a major network company, running a significant number of sales development workshops focused on live deals. The Power Base®[1] sales methodology was strong, customized to the client's business, and highly interactive in addressing real sales opportunities that each account executive was working on in the field. The evaluations were very positive and reflected the benefit of focusing on live deals in a very engaging and interactive manner. At the same time, conceptually sitting behind all of this was a Looking Glass Culture that was not entirely happy with the direction that Power Base® was taking the field sales organization. The client had been engaged in the acquisition of companies whose products consumed high amounts of bandwidth, as a complement to its focus on the network. The more bandwidth required, the more the network grew, and the more it grew, the more it drove the company's sales.

The CEO of this company was brilliant in building its end-to-end customer solutions. He knew the markets they served, and he spent around 60 percent of his time with customers. As we were working with the field, we spoke with him several times at the field offices as he was preparing for or coming back from account visits. He was a major asset to the sales organization as an executive sponsor to important and large opportunities and major accounts. That said, if you asked their customer executives about the primary focus of their business, the typical response would be that they're the router company.

So, while they had a strong end-to-end solution story for customers, the reality was that account executives were only calling on the IT groups in their customer companies. In truth, it was worse than that. They were often only calling on the network department *within* the IT

---

1   Power Base® is a registered trademark of HOLDEN LLC.

group. For them, the customer was not the company; the customer was the network group *within* the company.

This myopic view of customers was systemic within the sales organization. It affected everyone: the account executives, technical support people, sales managers, and executives—all the way up to but not including the CEO. In my view, he lived above the Looking Glass Culture and probably assumed that everyone was on board with the end-to-end solution concept. However, they were not, and this is an example of how strong and well-intentioned company executives can be ineffective in managing culture, as they are unknowingly shut off from the reality of their organization at the street level.

Because of all the acquisitions, the organization consisted of many versions of a Looking Glass Culture that did not play well together. The end-to-end solutions looked great in theory, but to operationalize them within accounts required strong internal collaboration to form expanded and integrated client-specific solutions. And that never really happened, as each acquisition had its own culture.

The ability to see and understand this is why sellers can be so effective in driving shifts in culture. It is also why the best place to begin enhancing a company culture is in the sales organization. What happens there can reach back to all facets of the company and its culture, as sales is an integrated function within a company. Sellers can look into their own company while also looking into customer organizations and observing the mirror reflection of their company culture from the customer perspective. What they see is cause and effect, enabling them to connect cultural norms to sales activities and customer response. They also instinctively know that for any cultural change to occur there must be clear visibility into what's really happening as well as a recognition of its relevant value. For sellers, that value is winning a deal, getting paid commission, and being recognized for good work. The latter contributes to future success in that value recognition by the right people drives access to more company resources. In turn, more deals are won. So, how might this connection between company sales culture to sales activity and customer response look from an operational and practical point of view?

Let's take a look at an example where the seller is the pursuit lead on an important opportunity. This seller, let's call her Elaine, is experienced and has qualified the opportunity to establish that it's real. She knows a deal will happen, when it will probably happen, what it represents in terms of revenue, and what it will take to pursue the opportunity in terms of business development expense and manpower. Elaine also knows that there is no crystal ball in selling, but she has a rationale to support the qualification of the opportunity based upon research on the account and discussions with the customer. As an example, she didn't just ask when a purchase decision would likely be made; she went deeper to get beyond a surface response.

Perhaps Elaine said something like, "I appreciate your input on timing, but what are the consequences of not making a decision at that time?" And, she didn't stop there. She also may have asked, "What could cause a delay in decision timing? For example, has the budget been approved for the acquisition?" With a green light on qualification and sales management approval of business development funding for the pursuit, Elaine then forms her pursuit team and begins to plan out the sales campaign.

As the customer buying process has been formally structured, the customer has allocated a time for each supplier to ask questions as part of a due diligence effort. Each supplier will have time to present their preliminary thinking on a solution to address the customer's needs based upon the customer Request For Proposal (RFP). There will also be time to ask questions and build further insight into the customer's business. For the pursuit lead, a lot of work has gone into preparing for this event. However, the day before the customer meeting, Elaine gets a call from one of her senior executives who asks for an update on the campaign. She briefs him and welcomes his support and interest. The problem is that he insists on a change in the solution that she knows will not be well received by the customer. What does she do? Does Elaine create conflict with her executive who has given her a directive? Or, does she disregard the directive and do what she believes is right and risk her job? What would you do?

You see, this question is not about sales methodology or sales skills or sales compensation; it's about sales culture and the political influence that drives it. Do the cultural inhabitants in this company get rewarded for taking a risk, or is getting along more important, even if it means losing business? Is courage and conviction to do the right thing for the customer important, recognized, and rewarded? In a Client-Centric Culture, it is. In a Looking Glass Culture, it is not.

Client-Centric Cultures lead to trust-based relationships with customers, reflecting on the suppliers as partners rather than vendors. This creates sellers who are more like consultants who are being paid to provide clients with value—not to sell stuff, per se, but to drive the sale and oversee the delivery of value having defeated competitors. It's a different mindset and selling orientation, operating at a higher level of professionalism and reflecting strong integrity even if it means taking on some personal and political risk. Sellers in a Client-Centric Culture are leaders who know how to manage risk and be client-specific with solutions and services even when engaged in large commodity deal pursuits.

So now, let me ask the question again. What would you do if you were the pursuit lead in our example? Your answer will indicate who you really are as a person. If you are going to put the customer's interest first and manage the political risk, my next question is, "Will your company support you?" The answer to that will indicate if you are living in a Client-Centric Culture or a Looking Glass Culture. If it's the latter, what are you prepared to do about it?

Your options are to comply with the executive directive and culture; resolve the conflict of the directive and become a vanguard for sales culture change, working to shift the culture; or leave the company. Recognize that leaving is not necessarily a defeatist approach. Sometimes change will only occur when one person takes a stand and convinces others to join based upon what is right, along with being fully prepared to leave if necessary. Building a critical mass of support for all the right reasons in the field sales organization, including that of a supportive sales manager, can effect cultural change when the value argument is strong enough. I certainly don't mean that you should be threatening the company, but rather you should work with sales management to connect lost business to the sales culture.

This is the bold and constructive approach to achieving the goal of winning the battle and growing in strength: doing what is right for the client, winning the business, and improving the sales culture that will help others win deals, as well. If culture does one thing well, it scales the impact of its norms. This creates the potential to drive overall company growth and success. But a seller cannot do this alone.

Establishing a Unified Customer Focus

The best way to change culture is to create a unified focus on clients, actioned by powerful people from within the company. This is change not by force through authority, policy, or inducing fear, but through leadership that resides at many levels—leadership that casts a client-facing vision, sets operational direction, and emphasizes value. That is what Satya Nadella, CEO of Microsoft, focused on when he set Microsoft on a course for change. As a catalyst, he took the powerful Microsoft and made it better by shifting its inward focus to that of customers and their success. Excerpts from Nadella's Inspire Ready 2018 presentation to the Microsoft community reflect this.[2]

It was during that presentation, after commenting on the company's 2018 success, that Nadella said, "But what binds us together, though, is not our success, it's the success that our customers achieve, because that's what makes us as a community, as a tech ecosystem, unique, different." He later went on to say, "Growth mindset is the meme we picked for that continuous process of renewal. And it's not about reaching some destination. We are about continuously, in fact, confronting our fixed mindset. The idea is not to celebrate any progress here, it is about being able to acknowledge the imperfection that

---

2 news.microsoft.com/uploads/prod/2018/07/07182018-Inspire-Ready-Satya-Nadel-laSC.docx

each of us has, starting with me, and to be able to ask ourselves: Are we doing everything we can when it comes to being obsessed about customers?"

A "meme" is a central organizing cultural practice that is key to a specific culture; one that is repeated often and evidenced by actions that support it. In Nadella's case, it was continuous renewal of the organization, acknowledging Microsoft's imperfections and those in himself as the company's leader. Gone was the arrogance of the past, with humility and honesty now taking the cultural lead. He went on to say, "We need to break free of any past dogma of any category, any business model, so that we can come together as one company and one ecosystem to really meet the needs of the customers. That's what this cultural process is all about. But, ultimately, though, the culture creates this amazing platform for us—at a time like this, where digital technology is part of every fabric of life and economy and society, to be able to connect with our own personal passions and philosophies, because that's what really enables us."

When Nadella talked about "confronting our fixed mindset" and the "need to break free of any past dogma," he is being consistent with the biblical principle of testing the environment to ensure that client success is the top priority. He has built a client-facing vision that sets operational direction for the entire organization.

Nadella's approach to shaping culture exists in sharp relief to that of a similar, but different, company and culture that reflected an entirely different set of values. It too was a large multinational firm where we had access to a senior executive and wanted sponsorship to the global head of sales. Thankfully, the meeting with the senior guy went well, and he gave us three options. Option one, as he presented it, was that he would set up a meeting with the sales lead for us and if it went well, it would significantly increase our business with them. Option two, we meet with the sales lead and it doesn't go well, meaning we get no future business. And, option three, we don't meet with the sales lead and continue to maintain our current level of business.

We chose option one with some confidence, as we had been running a series of ninety-minute opportunity coaching sessions to help account executives win business, and it had been going well. This is a service that we provide to many of our clients. So, when we briefed the sales lead, we expected to see some acknowledgement of the value provided. Instead, he stood up, raised his voice, and challenged how we could possibly accomplish anything in ninety minutes. And, by the way, if we did, why weren't his sales managers already doing it? It was like an explosion of social aggressiveness directed at me personally.

So, I stood up and in a clear, direct, but friendly voice, explained how we had seen specific patterns of sales behavior that we were prepared to address, which made our sales coaching process both effective and efficient. Being big on analytics (as I'm an engineer by schooling), we made our case and it was accepted. He smiled and sat down. From that point on the tone and outcome of the meeting was positive. But, what a ride! You see, challenge was part of the culture. His question about the sales managers was rhetorical. It was just about challenge.

Another expression of culture that we see with a number of companies is quarterly performance reviews that are based upon stack ranking. No matter how well people perform, if they are in the bottom percentile of performers, their performance is rated poor. As a result, when it comes to really important initiatives that require the best and brightest people, no one will want in. You could be super smart. You could be super committed. It doesn't matter because you would be competing for your job ranking with other super smart and committed individuals who could put you in the bottom ten percent. The challenge and personal risk is simply not manageable.

An example of this was published in a recent blog that reflects on pre-Nadella days at Microsoft, "At the center of Microsoft's cultural problem was their performance review system. Every manager was forced to place their employees on a scale from top to poor performers . . . . Executives reported that some of Microsoft's top engineers would avoid working alongside each other out of fear that they would be hurt in their rankings . . . . This created a culture of sabotage. Employees would work hard to achieve the best results, but, at the same time, they would try to ensure their colleagues did not."[3]

This same blog went on to say, "Microsoft executives couldn't understand why the company was struggling in the quality of its innovation compared with competitors such as Apple and Google. Endless surveys were conducted and every time the same answer would appear: Employees at Microsoft simply did not want to work together."[4]

Dial forward to Nadella's comments in Microsoft's 2019 annual report, "Over the past year, we have made progress in building a diverse and inclusive culture where everyone can do their best work. Since FY16, we have nearly doubled the number of women corporate vice

---

3   blog.impraise.com/360-feedback/microsoft-throws-stack-ranking-out-the-window
4   Ibid.

presidents at Microsoft—both overall and in technical roles. We've increased African American/Black and Hispanic/Latino representation by 33 percent. And this past fiscal year more than half of our U.S. interns were women or African American/Black and Hispanic/Latino. We must keep pushing to do more, and representation is only one measure of progress. Creating a diverse and inclusive workplace at Microsoft is everyone's job. And this year we increased our commitment, ensuring that every leader and employee prioritizes diversity and inclusion as part of our annual performance review process."[5]

Nadella has demonstrated great sensitivity and caring about the employees of Microsoft and reshaping its culture to be more focused on clients. It's an amazing start to a process that will now need to transfer that sensitivity to the employees themselves, and in particular, to sellers. To really create a Client-Centric Culture, the sellers will need to develop a high level of empathy and respect for clients, putting themselves in their clients' shoes. It's a sensitivity that acknowledges that clients live with risk as well, and that everything possible needs to be done to help them reduce that risk as it relates to your business. It's listening carefully and being both intellectually and emotionally committed to assisting them.

I had the good fortune to climb Mount Rainier a number of times. As I was first training on Nisqually Glacier for a week with Phil Ershler, an accomplished mountain climber and trainer, I began to develop my climbing philosophy. Somewhat similar to culture, it consisted of a set of principles to follow for high altitude technical mountaineering. These principles include:

---

5   www.microsoft.com/en-us/annualreports/ar2018/annualreport#primaryR1

- When in doubt chicken out. One of the first things Phil told me early on was that there is nothing romantic about dying on a mountain.
- Speed is safety. For me and my climbing team that meant not just moving fast but moving to safety.
- No bivouac equipment. I believed that if you don't have it, you can't use it. Therefore, we needed the best possible situational awareness of weather and mountain conditions, which meant knowing the mountain.

But to make this philosophy operational and effective required:

- *Sensitivity*—listening and watching everything, from looking back to know the way down to safety, to watching the freeze point as an indicator of avalanche potential, to signs of storm fronts, to listening to our bodies for physical and emotional issues. *Translation: Listen to the customer with sincerity to not only hear and understand what they need and are saying, but to know their culture and the values that define the company.*
- *Humility*—knowing that the mountain is king. It calls the shots. There is no place for ego on a mountain, no matter how successful or great you think you are—the mountain rules. *Translation: Respectfully recognize the authority of the customer.*

On my first ascent up Mount Rainier to summit, we needed to deal with an objective hazard. It was a 30-foot long ledge about 6 inches wide that stretched across an acute vertical that needed to be traversed. Below it was hundreds of feet to the bottom where we could see large rocks and blocks of ice that had fallen from high above us. The guide told us that rocks and ice continuously fall from the top and that we should cross ever so smoothly and carefully so as not to lose our footing or catch our 12-point crampons on our climbing boot gaiters. He advised our team—we were stacked up close to one another with climbing rope coiled up in our arms and connecting us—that if one went down, we all would go down. Then came the most important instruction: to listen very carefully. When rock or ice fall you can hear a slight whistling in the air as it travels downward at high speed. At that moment, everyone stops, leans in as close to the vertical wall of rock as possible, and says a prayer. No one looks down, no one checks their heart rate that's so fast it probably couldn't be measured, everyone listens and stops in unison, and everyone thinks: we're going to do this.

Listening and sensitivity became critical on another Mount Rainier climb. My team was on the upper mountain attempting a heavy climb with 80-pound backpacks and pulling sleds. It was a bright sunny day as we moved up the glacier when suddenly everything metal began to buzz. My ice axe, ice hammer, and everything with a metal point was buzzing. Without thought, delay, or discussion we dropped our loads and raced down to Camp Muir, a small wooden building, at 10,000-feet elevation. On a mountain, buzzing is the air ionizing, which can be a precursor to a lightning strike, even on a clear day. With 12-point steal crampons locked into the ice, if lighting strikes it's not going to be a good day for anyone on the glacier. For me, it was these kinds of experiences that made really clear the importance of treating the mountain with respect, demonstrating high sensitivity to everything—

listening, watching, and sensing anything that was even remotely out of place or unusual—and then acting or moving in the right direction without hesitation and with team unity of thought and action. But all this begins with respect for the mountain; just as in sales there must be respect for the client.

Respect for the client is critical to serving them well by checking at the door anything that could get in the way. Ego, internal supplier politics, culture, career issues, generic messaging, and everything else that is internally risk-oriented need to be out of mind when working with and serving clients. What matters first are the client's needs and risks they are facing, and how you will address those needs to produce significant business value, while reducing both personal and professional risk for every client contact to the extent possible.

Summary of Chapter 3

In this chapter, you've seen that culture is shaped and maintained by the collective control of powerful individuals where influence, not authority, rules. A CXO may think of the culture as being one thing when it's really another. Still, executives, sales managers, and sellers can initiate culture change, and the latter especially can connect cultural norms to sales activities to client responses, seeing the forest through the trees. You've also seen the sales dilemma, in our Elaine example, when internal cultural norms are violated to better serve a customer. If you are a seller, you're in a unique position to drive sales and play a key role in shifting your company culture, which we'll address in depth in the next chapter.

4

Why Sales

"In periods where there is no leadership, society stands still.
Progress occurs when courageous, skillful leaders seize the
opportunity to change things for the better."—Harry S Truman

What is the compelling argument for cultural change to operationally begin in the sales organization? There are five reasons why sellers are in the perfect position to effect change.

Proximity, Value, and Relevance—Nothing happens until someone sells something. Revenue is tied to sales and sales are tied to clients. And the closest people to clients are sellers. That makes clients important, but not just for the obvious revenue and margin. *Clients are the mirror reflection of a company's sales culture.* And that reflection will be right side up if your company culture is a Client-Centric Culture or upside down if it's a Looking Glass Culture. Sellers look it right in the face. There is no ambiguity. There is no confusion about the lack of face-to-face time with customers, sales forecasts that keep slipping, the use of one-size-fits-all proposals and presentations that are generic, the lack of understanding of the customer's business, the limited single thread account coverage, the shrinking pipeline, and more. This is where sellers need to be *in* the sales culture, by definition, but not *of* it—if it's a Looking Glass Culture.

They are agents for change if senior management will support them, which is why new CXO management often is required to start the process or support it when the field demonstrates conviction and boldness to initiate cultural change. How do you change the direction of a beam of light? You do it with a mirror, adjusting the mirror to send the light in the right direction. That's what the customer mirror can do. It can point your sales culture in the right direction. As simple as it sounds, all it requires is an honest and objective view of the customer and their response to sales activities. Counterproductive cultural norms are displaced by new, productive, and healthy ones.

During my first trip to Egypt to visit certain architectural digs I quickly noticed large mirrors at the outside of digs. They were accompanied by other mirrors at various points down deep and dark passageways to the actual excavation points. It was all about naturally illuminating the darkest and most precious part of the dig. The same is true with using the client as a mirror to reflect a company's culture through the sales force, shining a light onto counterproductive cultural norms that can otherwise be so difficult to see. One at a time, the change out of norms occurs, as each sales situation is an opportunity for new thinking and values to influence relationship building with accounts.

Perhaps the most fundamental of these values is expressed in: "And as you wish that others would do to you, do so to them" (Luke 6:31). Putting clients first is probably the most important norm and defining characteristic of a healthy and productive company culture. But, it's never easy. As mentioned earlier, a culture will destroy or purge itself of whatever it doesn't want to accept. Remember the monkeys we spoke of earlier and how they would band together to stop the one new thinker from trying to get the banana? This means that sellers and sales managers need to be strong and persistent, demonstrating conviction and boldness in the face of cultural resistance.

Conviction is believing even in the absence of proof, as evidenced by your actions. But just believing that customers should come first is one thing. It's quite another to go against the culture and perhaps against your senior management . . . maybe even putting your job on the line. Risk-averse people simply will not do it. But even those who will, need the strength of their convictions. They need to be bold. *If conviction is believing even in the absence of proof, as evidenced by your actions, conviction and boldness together is believing in the absence of proof, as evidenced by your actions irrevocably.* But recognize that you may need to stand alone during challenging times, for few people possess real conviction and boldness when facing adversity.

On one occasion when I had to demonstrate such conviction and boldness, I had just returned from an assignment in the mountains of Columbia working with a major computer company in Cali. As malaria had been reported there, I took a chloroquine-based med for protection, only to find myself experiencing chest pain upon returning to the States. Turned out that I was one of the 4 percent of users for whom the med could actually induce a heart attack. Fortunately, I had stopped taking it, but I quickly found myself in the ICU of a local hospital for a week. At the end of that time, I asked the heart specialist if I had had a heart attack. She responded by saying, "We don't know." My primary care guy advised me to simply avoid doing anything stressful and sent me home.

Feeling somehow "broken" I could not live with that advice. So, I trained for six months and climbed the highest mountain I could find that didn't require technical skills. It was Mt. Kilimanjaro at 19,340-feet elevation. My mission was to test myself. If I had a weak heart it would likely present itself on the summit attempt that took eleven hours with no food, little water, and no sleep the night before (as it turned out). If I didn't have a heart problem on the mountain, I would forget about it, which I did.

Now, I'm not advising this testing method for anything or anyone. But, while I might have been wrong or selfish with this test, I was not confused. It was go or no go. That was a decision that I made alone. And if you have to go up against bad culture to do what's right, you will likely stand alone, as well. It's part of not being risk-averse, believing in yourself not because you're strong, but because your faith, your conviction, is strong. It's being a leader, which is a big part of successful selling. That said, the operative word is, "believing," which is why I quote the Bible.

We all have some type of moral constitution and a conscience that reflects what we believe to be right in the eyes of God. If you're going to put your job on the line, you'll need to reach deep into your heart and know that putting customers first is right and that it matters. You may take some heat, and probably will, but I tell you that you will likely never feel so good about yourself and what you're doing for your company and clients. Believing in putting clients first is the basis for a trusting relationship with them, and trust is the critical basis for partnership:

From where does the belief come,

And where does the boldness lie?

With trust they move as one,

Like birds together they fly.

It's interesting to note that the words "trust" and "believe" come from the same Greek root (*pisteuo*). This is why real partnerships are so rare. As sellers, sales managers, and corporate executives, you can help build real client partnerships that have real meaning, and at the same time, you can strengthen sales culture and drive business in a way that brings fun, fulfillment, and satisfaction into sales. This will reach back and influence the entire company culture over time.

Face-to-Face Client Time. As Regina Brett says, "Most of life is showing up." It's all about time and what you do with time. But if you don't have time, what you do with it really doesn't matter. What we see today with the general decline of sales effectiveness is not the need for the latest sales methodology or account planning process or new sales techniques or psychology, but the need for appropriately managed time. The flood of emails that sellers receive every day, and all the compliance requirements that are imposed on them, contribute to an inward focus that is at the direct expense of client face-to-face time—making the job not just hard, but often impossible. Yet, because time is intangible and the presence of sellers in accounts is not visible to company management, the problem goes unrecognized or discounted.

In our view, sellers should be spending roughly four days a week in the field working with clients. One day a week is for planning, preparing, resourcing, and administration. That puts a serious curb on spending hours reading emails, filling out CRM forms, and other tasks that all have meaning, but may not be directly relevant to that which is expected of a seller, in terms of sales results.

This is where a really good sales manager comes in, working out an approach with the seller to insure that the stuff the seller really *does* need to be attentive to is allowed through, while all else is filtered out or parked with the support of the sales manager, who also takes the heat for running interference so that the seller can focus and do the job that is expected by the company.

For this to actually occur, the sales manager must also have conviction and boldness to defeat all the forms of cultural resistance that will work to contain, discourage, and possibly threaten him or her. It's not a job for the risk averse or weak hearted in today's world. Sales managers have responsibility for the numbers, but they may not have the political horsepower, drive, or ability to take responsibility for the means by which the numbers are actually produced.

Nevertheless, if their only contribution is to free up seller time, that is a significant accomplishment. What we see all too often today is arbitrage sales management where managers are getting information from sellers and just reporting it up without ever impacting the seller's ability to perform and produce better numbers. These people are dead wood in a Looking Glass Culture. But they get along really well with others internally. They're often viewed as team players, leading by informal committee, seeking a kind of organizational harmony, and are fundamentally nice people. But that is not what sellers in today's world need, particularly in a gig culture.

Access to Resources. When sellers have the right support it increases their sales effectiveness and their capacity. There is no substitute for having strong talented people by your side during an important and competitive sales campaign and during client fulfillment, which drives client satisfaction and additional business. But, when sellers are living in a Looking Glass Culture and are resistant to that culture for all the right reasons, they are often not viewed as being "team players." This is because the culture is a get-along culture where inward focus and customer insensitivity is rewarded with acquiesce and tolerance, even though the lack of sales results is frustrating to management. Seems inconsistent, right? Welcome to the irrational world of the Looking Glass Culture. And when a seller does put the customer first and actually drives success, it can often be viewed by cultural inhabitants as a highly disruptive anomaly, to a point where they actually reduce resource availability to the seller going forward. It's right back to our monkeys and the regrettable monkey mindset of a Looking Glass Culture.

Being Relevant. The best way to work toward a Client-Centric Culture and do the job well as a seller is to be viewed by senior company management as advancing, either directly or indirectly, the right corporate executive priorities. Just as is done in accounts to position solution value with clients, so too is there a need to be connected to the right executives and the right priorities internally. For example, if the sale and client success of a new product that could open a new market for the company through new competitively differentiated innovation is achieved, the value of the sale essentially exceeds the revenue generated. It takes on strategic value relative to driving future sales through the development of a new market, thus creating new sources of revenue.

This will be important to the product manager, finance, operations, and senior management, but it's also important that these people know *who* sold the business and what was done to make it happen, particularly if it was countercultural. Over time the seller will build a support base within the company that will increase his or her influence, access to resources, and will help the sales manager run interference when necessary. Think of it as building your influence inventory within the company. It will also be important in terms of culture change, as senior executives recognize and understand the commitment and ability of the seller and want to replicate and scale it. That desire to replicate is the seed for cultural transformation.

Discerning the Political Landscape. Mapping out the political landscape within accounts is not easy and all too often sellers can confuse friendly supporting contacts with powerful client individuals. It's human nature to hear what we want to hear as we discover the distribution of influence vs. authority within our client organizations. That said, one of the best ways to develop political acumen is to build it within your own company where you have a lot more information to guide you. It also tells you who to be "relevant" to within product management, finance, operations, and senior management, which we discussed earlier. Some individuals within these company functions will have significantly more influence than others, both inside their organizations and across departmental lines. The principle is that

Value + Recognition = Power. Power is able to command resources, work in exception to culture, and to change culture. But that requires value recognition by the right people.

Summary of Chapter 4

In this chapter, you've seen the five reasons why sellers are in the most significant position to effect culture change, while also driving revenue. It's a compelling argument in that even CEOs that can initiate culture change cannot sustain it without a healthy and supporting sales culture that is driven by sellers in the field. In our next chapter we'll discuss how building your political acumen will be important to driving cultural change in the midst of winning important deals. Coupled with the right timing and entrepreneurial ability, building a support base of powerful individuals will place you in a strong leadership position to drive change, while securing important business.

PART TWO

A Deep Dive into Culture

5

Culture and Politics

"Only three things happen naturally in organizations: friction, confusion, and underperformance. Everything else requires leadership."—Peter Drucker

Cultural change is all about leadership, political power, timing, and entrepreneurial ability. And this begins with mapping out your company's political landscape to create a support base for cultural change—just as you would do in accounts to win important deals. Without it, your efforts to change culture and secure significant opportunities will be like rolling a big rock uphill. It will be fatiguing, frustrating, and futile. Building political insight means letting go of old thinking where authority principally defines an organization, and recognizing that influence and authority are not the same.

While influence is often derived from authority, not all people who have authority will have influence. A senior executive soon to retire will likely have little influence on major decisions. Or, an individual with authority may have influence in some areas of the business and not in others. Conversely, a person with little authority may have significant influence based upon an association with authority. That is, a trust-based relationship with a senior executive may enable a lower-level person to have and exert influence. In some cases, the lower level individual may look like an informal proxy, as others infer that the person is representing the executive's view on a particular subject.

An example of this can be seen with an outside advisor, hired by a company to manage the procurement process for a major acquisition. An entire industry has grown up in this area largely due to the growing cultural dysfunction that we see in field sales and the misalignment it creates with client cultures. The consultant has no authority but operates pretty much with the same level of influence as the executive who hired him or her, relative to the acquisition. In other cases, it is simply understood that a lower-level person has a relationship with a particular senior executive which gives that person access to and the ability to influence the executive. Anyone wanting to be on the good side of the executive will not want to be in conflict with the lower-level individual. It's just human nature.

What's not human nature is prioritizing the intangible above the tangible. If it's not real and physical, the tendency of a lot of people is to discount its significance. Yet, we know that generally speaking the intangibles rule. Take something as simple as a conversation with a client. It's not what you say, or even what you think the client heard that's really important. It's how the client feels that matters. Is the client emotionally engaged and supportive, or disinterested, or perhaps even sees you as a threat in some way? So it is with influence: it's an intangible that is only visible when it is being exerted.

We view organizational politics as a Power Base, the influential body within an organization. Think of this group as a social network sitting on a professional platform. It is made up of influential people who communicate frequently and who share common values. As such, it is not only a powerful network of people, but also one with its own subculture that tends to shape the environment around it. Unlike an organization chart that clearly and tangibly identifies individuals, their positions, and level of authority, the Power Base is not visible and only becomes so when its members are exerting influence, particularly across department lines in areas where the Power Base members have no actual authority. It is important to these people that their level of influence not be recognized, as they could be viewed as usurping the authority of others. Accordingly, one of the unspoken norms of a Power Base culture is concealment. When influence is exerted it is only for a moment, like a flash of light illuminating power and then going dark.

Whenever humans are interacting as a group with some purpose or mission, a social order is formed to establish and maintain stability and leadership. It could be a company business unit or the Parent Teacher Association (PTA). Generally, it consists of some formal structure that defines roles and authority, along with its informal culture. Both the formal and informal shape the social order and behavior. *In a Power Base, there is no formal component to the social order, only that of influence and culture where the culture provides stability and influence provides power.*

Leadership resides with one person whom we symbolize as a Fox. This person is the center of influence and all others in the Power Base derive their power by association with him or her. Foxes are not like most people. They are not easy to spot unless you know very well what to look for in an organization.

In the wild, foxes are not like pack animals that are loud, noisy, and very visible. Instead, they live in small families, hunting at night when they are not very visible and traveling wherever they need to go, including up trees. This is akin to our Foxes operating up, down, and across organizational lines. In fact, real foxes have such a wide range of travel and are so adaptable that they are considered an invasive species. Scientists tell us that foxes can see the earth's magnetic field and use it to navigate and hunt. Power Base Foxes also see the intangible, but in their case the intangible is influence. A Fox can spot powerful people and another Fox within an organization a long way off.

In the wild, foxes are creative and disciplined. When chased by a predator, a fox will run in large circles, trading off with its mate. When the predator stops from exhaustion, the foxes just walk away. When confronted with fleas, the fox doesn't bite and scratch, but instead looks for a lake. He takes a stick in his mouth and begins to swim. As fleas apparently don't like water, they migrate up the fox's back, up his neck and over his head to the stick. After a while the fox just lets the stick go, along with all the fleas.

But foxes are not people. They don't possess the ability to make moral choices; Power Base Foxes do have this ability. And for them, based upon our observations across companies, industries, and geography over time, they have the trait of integrity. Foxes put their companies first, ahead of themselves, and never work to advance themselves at the expense of their companies.

A Jackal, on the other hand, looks like a fox but is not. He is a scavenger and a very different animal. In a company, when you spot a very powerful individual with strong influence, but also with a willingness to advance his or her own interests at the expense of the company, he is not a Fox, but a Jackal. And, if there is one thing we can say about corporate Jackals, it is to stay far away from them. You may be tempted to align with such a person in the pursuit of an important deal, particularly if that individual opposes your competition. But be aware that the idea "the enemy of my enemy is my friend" has not worked out well in the past. While many nation-states have employed it, rarely has it been successful in the long term.

For alignment to be successful, it must be based on trust. And that will not exist with Jackals. If they are willing to sacrifice their company, they will be willing to sacrifice you to protect or advance themselves. Over time their actions always find them out, but before that happens they can do a lot of damage to a lot of people. In the world of organizational politics, it's important to find the Foxes, but more important to find and avoid the Jackals. Fortunately, there are far fewer Jackals than Foxes in my experience, but sell long enough in the B2B space and you will for sure run into one at some point. When that happens, you'll see that one core attribute separates the two: trust.

If you look at a graph of performance on one axis and trust on the other, Foxes will reside at the medium to high levels of performance, along with a high level of trust. Jackals may be high performers but are low on trustworthiness. An example of this is seen when a manager with Fox-like power engages in a power struggle that degenerates into a power play. Power struggles are common to contention management cultures where they are considered healthy. But, not so for power plays, as the driver of a power play is often quite willing to sacrifice the company to gain advantage in the power play, making them parasitic. The people who engage in such activity don't wear black hats or hooded sweatshirts. On the contrary, they suit up well and look like Foxes, but they are manipulative in nature. They are Jackals.

Beware, beware,
Looks can deceive.
What will appear,
Is not to believe.

If a powerful individual should ask you to share your opinion of another executive to a more senior person with whom you have a good relationship or to comment on a new initiative being proposed by another manager, recognizing that you have a dim view of the project, what should be your response? With ego in check, a safe response is along the lines of, "We'll support whatever your company feels is appropriate." The guideline here is to always stay on the edge of client politics, aware of it and aligning with the right powerful people, but never becoming involved in the politics itself—and always be aware of Jackals who could draw you into the fray. Interestingly the biblical parallel to this we see in Jeremiah 49:33: "Hazor will become a haunt of jackals, a desolate place forever. No one will live there; no people will dwell in it," (NIV) and "Hazor shall be a dwelling for dragons, and a desolation forever: there shall no man abide there, nor any son of man dwell in it" (KJV). While the translations from the original Hebrew word differ (jackal and dragon), they both carry a negative connotation, from a jackal symbolizing desolation to a dragon referring to Satan, as we see in the New Testament. Whatever the exact translation, jackals are to be avoided.

Foxes are an asset to any company in that they provide both formal and informal leadership throughout an organization with a minimum of bureaucracy, which is particularly important when formal leadership channels get bogged down. So, what do we know about Foxes in terms of descriptive traits?

- **Results Oriented** – Foxes do not engage in busy work or confuse activity with results. For example, if asked about specific accomplishments while in a particular role, their response would never center on how many countries had been visited or miles flown.

- **Situationally Aware** – Foxes know what's going on throughout the company and are rarely surprised by events. For example, they will know about a reorganization in advance.

- **Able to Work in Exception to Policy** – Foxes build trust-based relationships with key people so that when an exception to policy is required—for example, hiring someone during a hiring freeze—it is rarely questioned. This acknowledges that no policy is perfect and that exceptions can be appropriate, particularly when made by Foxes who are known for their ability, intent, and character.

- **Calculated Risk Takers** – Foxes balance and manage risk, even in crises. They look at both the magnitude and manageability of risk relative to potential gain. For example, if the risk is moderate and the manageability of risk is high—meaning that any problem that might develop will be visible early and the means to mitigate risk in real time will be straight forward—a Fox would likely proceed with the initiative if justified by the potential return.

- **Strong Delegators** – Foxes by definition will delegate heavily to Power Base members. For example, when influencing a decision in another department, a Fox may work through a Power Base member who will contact an individual in the other department, with whom he or she has a good relationship, to discuss an issue and perhaps make an informal recommendation.

- **Great Listeners** – Foxes don't usually speculate without good reason, but instead they gather intel at every opportunity, listening and thinking at every turn. Foxes listen well to establish and maintain good situational awareness. This enables them to ask good questions that communicate understanding and caring. They engender a sense or feeling in others that they are, "one of us." To support this, they keep speaking to a minimum, listening and mostly asking questions, and rarely expressing a view or taking a position on an issue unless it is judged appropriate. Instead, they often work through the informal network to influence an outcome without being personally associated with the outcome, which could be the case if a position had been declared. Foxes are masters of the indirect approach and use it frequently.

- **Humble** – For Foxes, humility is more than a nice human trait. They know the danger of ego and how it can grow through success into hubris. As an excess of arrogance, hubris promotes an insensitivity to reality and detail, while dramatically increasing a sense of self-worth that can easily become self-defeating. Napoleon's early military success was under the guidance of Sun Tzu's book *The Art of War*. In fact, the first translation was in French. But then he got to the point where he apparently felt he knew better or perhaps didn't want to be constrained by Sun Tzu's principles. His defeat in 1812 during the invasion of Russia was not due to Russian military superiority, but rather to the weather. His army of half a million men was defeated by snowflakes. Humility requires self-awareness and strength and once mastered is a source of power.

- **Change Agents** – Arguably one of the most significant Fox-like traits is that of being a force for change. Foxes produce results and value everywhere they operate. They are always on a mission to create some kind of value for the company and others, as they are generally givers, not takers, in life. But they are also savvy enough to know that value plus recognition equals power. So, they are careful to be recognized by the right people, relative to the right outcomes, and to maintain an appropriately low profile with everyone else. As the right people include other Foxes, individuals in the Power Base, and high level executives, Foxes are in a good position to drive changes in business models and direction, priorities, the organization, and its culture. As big as Microsoft is, I would bet that Satya Nadella could still tell you where a Fox resides in each major area of Microsoft—and more than that, how he involved those Foxes in his vision, direction, and priorities for the company.

Building Your Client Influence Inventory

How do you align with a client Power Base to build influence? When I first began selling to a major telecommunications company in the Midwest, I was told by the product manager of my company's board test division not to attempt to sell any of our board testers, as the client was committed to buying both HP and Tektronix systems. They had software engineers trained in programming, an inventory of hardware fixtures, lots of spares for maintenance, and from a business point of view, good risk management with two suppliers. There simply was no need for a third and it was the preference of our product manager that I focus on other more viable accounts.

That said, we did sell other equipment to the account and one day I was approached to bid on a board test application, but only to comply with a new purchasing policy of having at least three suppliers bid for large dollar procurements. The senior engineer was clear that it was a courtesy request and that they did not foresee any changes in suppliers. And that was okay with me, as I knew that I could never win the business if I took a traditional approach. But conventional thinking and traditional selling was not what I had in mind.

Immediately, I began doing my homework and researching the account only to find that HP and Tektronix had been doing a great job and were well respected. Clearly a direct strategy focused on solution superiority was out. I had to go indirect with a new and nontraditional source of competitive advantage. And it had to be a sales approach that included a force multiplier or asymmetric advantage that was disproportionately greater than what my competition would expect from us. They had the installed base, connections with management, and the trust of the engineers who had to make the equipment work in a manufacturing environment. They had superiority, but if I played it right, I would have the element of surprise.

It was then that I began to really see organizational influence vs. authority based on how people were communicating both inside and outside the group making the buy. It turned out that the department chief, whom the senior engineers reported to, was very involved in a new software system to support manufacturing in accordance with quality principles espoused by people like Edward Deming who pioneered new thinking in quality management. It didn't take long to see that this department chief had a strong reputation and the support of senior management. He was clearly a Fox who was on a mission to transform how his company manufactured sophisticated electronic systems.

With this research and understanding, I had the basis for my indirect sales strategy. I would change the ground rules from board testing alone to board testing that would advance the new manufacturing software that had been developed under the direction of the department chief. We formed the solution quietly involving our software engineers, in order to interface with the new manufacturing software, which became the focus of my presentation. Each supplier was given an hour and a half to present their solution and I was last in. But, while my competition used up the ninety minutes, I was done in about a half hour. There were no questions and the engineers didn't understand why I was talking so much about the manufacturing process and software that was clearly out of scope. But for them, it didn't really matter, as I was just a "procurement compliance" bidder. So, they were polite and before long I was on the way back to my office.

As I walked in, my sales manager's admin advised me that the department chief, who had sat in on the presentation, was on the phone. Curious, I picked up my phone and said, "Hello, this is Jim Holden."

The response was devoid of pleasantry as the chief simply said, "I want you to know that I know what you're doing. And, that I support it." At that, he hung up. Two days later, I got a call from one of his senior engineers advising us that we had won the bid. Two days after that, HP was in the account and asked the same senior engineer why on earth they had decided to go with us? His response, as he described it to me, was, "We don't know. But the decision has been made by management and we will make it successful." That's when I physically saw the power of political alignment and building a client inventory of influence as a nontraditional source of competitive advantage.

Types of Power Bases

There are two types of Power Bases: organizational and situational. Every company business unit, division, and department will have an organizational Power Base, and in addition, there will be a corporate executive Power Base at the top of the organization. Generally speaking, these Power Bases reside within, and are defined by, the organizational scope of their groups and are often quite stable.

A situational Power Base, on the other hand, is created when something important is occurring. It may be a major procurement, a restructuring of the business, or perhaps a contemplated buy, sell, or merger. It can also develop when an informal effort is being put forth to drive cultural change. Just as every formal procurement process will have assigned decision makers, it will also have an informally structured situational Power Base that may or may not be decision makers. But, as influence flows mainly out of a Power Base and not into it, decision makers will be influenced by the situational Power Base. When driving cultural change, the influence is on company individuals who are in positions to support the pursuit campaign for a large deal. Unlike an organizational Power Base, a situational one will be very fluid, changing over time, particularly when a pursuit campaign needs different forms of support, from customization of a solution to changes in the company's business model. This suggests that constant monitoring and updating to know who is moving in and out of a situational Power Base is required. It also means that the pursuit lead will need to work with Foxes to ensure that the right people are involved in supporting the pursuit at the right time.

A sales example of the need to stay on top of political developments came up when I was doing a review of a major sales campaign within a very large account, which was an industry-leading insurance company in Belgium. The pursuit team had done a good job over a period of about eighteen months, understanding the customer, developing an excellent solution to consolidate IT and outsource it to improve productivity and reduce cost, and had built and run a traditional sales campaign, with reasonable competitive differentiation. They were down selected from many to just a few as the sales situation advanced and was peaking.

The situational Fox was the CEO who had then made a request for a discount on the front-end consulting engagement. The pursuit team, wanting to be responsive, accommodated the request by providing the discount, but also adding a performance bonus on the back-end outsourcing effort, as an offset to the discount. The CEO then stated that he would support whatever decision was made by his senior team that included his country presidents. For him, the financial risk of the acquisition was significantly reduced and so he essentially exited the situational Power Base.

Very quickly the German country lead became the situational Fox and he didn't support the centralization of IT, as he wanted to maintain control if IT in Germany. Other country leads quickly agreed with him and the deal was killed. This underscores the need to stay on top of the situational Power Base and always apply "what if" thinking to every important sales campaign decision that's being made, particularly post down select. It's during this time that the deck of cards will be reshuffled, making you the most vulnerable to a change in your client influence inventory.

Moments of Truth

There is a time when a Looking Glass Culture can no longer be tolerated by high performing sellers. This occurs when a moment of truth emerges; a time when the presence of a Looking Glass Culture is about to destroy a qualified and important pursuit. Yellow flashing warning signs emerge at the customer interface, as your sales culture finds the following to be acceptable and expected:

- Generic proposals and presentations, often part of a unified messaging effort;
- A lack of clear understanding of the customer's business, such as their vision, direction, and priorities;
- Value that is not positioned to advance customer executive priorities either directly or indirectly, perhaps focused on operational value and cost reduction;
- Political alignment that really doesn't exist, such as when a friendly supporter is mistaken for the situational Fox;
- The pursuit team is leading by committee.

These moments are not only the signposts for change; they are clear warnings that the sales organization is becoming dysfunctional. Sales will decline, win rates will drop, pipeline volume will shrink, and sales forecasting will become more and more inaccurate. As such, it is in the best interest of sellers, sales managers, and executives to support change. But that will rarely happen. As the saying goes, "They can't see the forest for the trees." And when you live in a particular culture it's not easy to see the effects of that culture, as the cultural norms shape one's thoughts and actions. If you are paying attention and recognize the moments of truth, you will see the need for change, but most others will not.

That's why it's important to narrow your focus to the Power Base within the field sales organization. Socialize the rational for change with people who have the ability to see the intangible, which is generally the case with Power Base members who see and possess influence, as an intangible. They will likely not discount the moments of truth that you have experienced and will comprehend their significance. Your goal is to help form a situational or, more specifically, a cultural Power Base in the field for cultural change with a Fox taking the lead. The Fox will have the power and executive access to bring the message to senior leadership and begin the process for change. But for this to happen, you need to have real leadership ability that comes with being an effective seller, sales manager, or executive. As such, you can think of yourself as an entrepreneur—not in the sense of starting a new business, but in creating a new culture.

The Need for Entrepreneurship

The word *entrepreneur* is French, meaning one who undertakes a task that involves initiative and risk. And, as the catalyst for cultural change, you will need lots of initiative and will be taking on lots of risk. As we've said before, a culture will resist change, destroying or purging itself of anything it can't conform to itself or assimilate. Any culture will resist change with the power of a freight train. Its inertia is strong; its will even stronger. Get in its way and the outcome is certain. But surgically narrow your focus to the cultural Power Base, as in the track ahead, and you can derail bad culture. It's a divide-and-conquer effort by starting small and establishing a critical mass of influence to effect change. As cultural inhabitants oppose your efforts and defend the existing culture, you'll be facing the disruptive side of changing culture. But again, it can be managed by the cultural Power Base when initiated by your entrepreneurial spirit and leadership and supported by the Fox.

In 1980, the Wollman Skating Rink in New York broke and could not make ice, much to the frustration of 138,000 people who used it every year. The city of New York spent $13 million dollars over six years trying to fix it without success. Then, an entrepreneur whose office and apartment overlooked Central Park approached the mayor and offered to fix the problem. Frustrated, the mayor gave this individual $3 million dollars and six months to get the job done. The difficulty was that the person didn't know anything about fixing ice skating rinks.

Recognizing this deficiency, as good entrepreneurs do in acknowledging their own shortcomings, he then proceeded to find the best ice skating rink company on the planet, which was a Canadian company that makes virtually all the National Hockey League skating rinks. After reviewing the problem, the company proposed a very straightforward solution that found itself at odds with what the city politicians wanted, which was reportedly much more complex. Nevertheless, the company was hired, and the entrepreneur literally inspected the progress every day. Ahead of schedule and $750,000 under budget, the work was completed. The $750,000 was then put in a trust for rink maintenance and a fee was charged to use the rink. Attendance jumped from 138,000 people per year to 256,000 per year, with profit from fee income also going into the trust to serve the community.[1]

This is a good example of how an entrepreneur solved a problem that the bureaucracy could not solve. In a company, the bureaucracy is part of the culture—it is created out of structure, culture, and process. *Therefore, a bureaucracy cannot change culture. A company trying to change its culture in the same way it would solve a business problem will fail.* It usually takes an entrepreneur like that of an enlightened and bold seller to initiate change, seeing and understanding the problem during a moment of truth, and coalescing the best people to solve it with simplicity, while also overseeing the implementation of the solution. Who is in a better position to do this than the people who work with customers on the front lines, seeing the problems firsthand? Sellers can change sales practices one by one to effect cultural change with cultural Power Base support, showcasing sales results to others to create more support for future change.

---

1   Story taken from *The Art of the Deal* by Donald Trump.

The decline in sales effectiveness within companies today and the inability of the city of New York to solve the ice skating rink problem is not a phenomenon unique to those situations. *Culture contributing to bureaucracy that reinforces culture can be a dynamic of its own in any environment.* And one such environment that is contributing to the formation and resilience of Looking Glass Cultures in American companies is the source of new company employees. Young people, graduating from college, bring new blood and vitality to businesses, which is to be admired. With that comes new thinking that often challenges old norms, policies, and procedures, and therefore, culture. Again, this is not bad, but when their thinking is based upon ideology that is anti-American, anti-capitalism, anti-small government, and anti-individual freedom, that's a problem, particularly since college culture is a leading indicator for corporate and American culture. We'll talk more about this later in the next chapter as Charlie Kirk, Founder and Executive Director of Turning Point USA, provides us with an in-depth view of what is happening with American youth, not only relative to its impact on companies as the future workforce, but also on academia that has seen a continuous decline in student enrollments.

According to an article in *Inside Higher Ed*, by Paul Fain: "College enrollment in the U.S. has decreased for the eighth consecutive year, according to new data released Thursday by the National Student Clearinghouse Research Center" (May 30, 2019). Some say that it's because the labor market is strong, putting jobs ahead of education in the competition for students. Others contend that the student population is getting smaller or that specialization in sports creates college dependency on too narrow a market. Whatever the reason, colleges will not be quick to solve the problem.

Businesses strive to be successful with checks and balances and accountability in place. A company board looks out for shareholders, always checking to see if important decisions being made by senior management are accretive to shareholders. HR departments are on top of government compliance requirements for hiring and personnel management. Finance keeps an eye on the business from a quantitative financial perspective, managing all financial aspects of the business to keep it healthy and strong. Culture notwithstanding, a company is a well-oiled business system of checks and balances. Colleges, on the other hand, particularly the Ivy League schools that rank among the top private US universities, have endowments that are often fully funded, meaning that they are not likely to run out of money. Their leading professors are tenured, meaning that no one can fire them. And while their boards have authority and could technically close a school or fire a president, it just doesn't happen. Academic culture simply will not permit it. As such, they demonstrate little meaningful influence; often following the lead of college presidents in a rub-ber-stamp approval mode. But what both business and academia have in common is bureaucracy.

Academic institutions that have little to no checks and balances become a kind of closed structure with bureaucracy and culture inter-twined into a tight knot. This causes countercultural change to be very difficult. In the past, women going to college shored up enrollments, and then it was foreign students. Sports programs played a big role in attracting new students. But now, most universities with their highly structured organizations and cultures have really nowhere to grow. In a free enterprise system this opens them up to vulnerability through new technology that—coupled with entrepreneurship—could introduce competition through innovative educational transformation.

For the colleges that are able to think and operate more like businesses, this could mean opportunity, particularly if, for example, they were to acquire new companies or access to new technologies that are pioneering innovation in advanced learning. But could it work? Would the existing college culture destroy the entrepreneurial heart of such a company?

My experience mentoring students suggests that young adults today want more than an education and social interaction. They're looking for purpose and something to bring meaning to their lives. Biblical leadership teaches us that "the purposes of a person's heart are deep waters, but one who has insight draws them out" (Proverbs 20:5). Each of us is born with a purpose and calling that we sense in our hearts—a purpose in life that will make a difference in the world. It gives meaning to our lives, strength and courage to our actions, and joy that gets us through life's setbacks. But do our universities in America have this "insight" to help students find their purpose?

This is not about shifting to online delivery of classes to support social distancing. And it's not about a STEM (Science, Technology, Engineering, and Math) interdisciplinary approach to learning or even a STEAM emphasis that adds the Arts to the mix to merge creativity with intellect, such as is attempted in this book with the use of poetry. It's about learning transformation that captures and encourages the entrepreneurial imagination and spirit of students, impacting their lives by participating in the development of new innovation to make a difference.

Understanding what this actually means and shifting focus and culture will be key for the universities that want to stay ahead of new emerging trends. And like in business, it will take individuals with strong influence to drive a vision for change where they serve as a buffer between the existing college culture and the innovative entrepreneurship that reflects new and often conservative thinking. We see these buffers today. They exist in the new innovation centers that companies and university/company partnerships are forming today that have their own facilities, close to the colleges and companies, but often physically and culturally separated. They enjoy a degree of independence not unlike what existed between Hong Kong and China, as these new innovation centers live outside of university culture. Some such centers are to be admired and some are not. If they are genuinely focused on advancing businesses and industries in a fiscally and socially responsible manner to drive growth and create future jobs for students, while also providing students with purpose in life, they are good.

Still, it's important to recognize that you can't legislate or dictate innovation, which more often happens spontaneously in a garage through individual creativity and dedication. But what if that is not the case? Hong Kong, a British colony, was returned to China in 1997 on the assurance that the region would remain semiautonomous under a principle of "one country, two systems" with its own democratic judicial system. But more recently we see China's real intent to increase control over Hong Kong with more of a culture of communism and what appears to be a long-term agenda set on power and subjugation.

If college leadership's goal is simply to check off the innovation center box to attract students based upon an apparent interest in new thinking and capitalism, only to migrate later to the mainstream college socialist culture, the move is as calculated and deceptive as that of Chinese leadership. In Hong Kong, students are making the difference with nearly 40 percent of the 6,100 police arrests reported to be students. Will students make the difference in today's American colleges, leading the charge with leadership and entrepreneurial ability?

Summary of Chapter 5

Just as in winning important deals and developing major accounts, mapping out the political landscape of an organization is key to reshaping culture. In this chapter, you've been introduced to the different types of Power Bases, Foxes, and Jackals who (like Foxes) are powerful but dangerous to align with for so many reasons. In addition to the Fox-like traits of Results Oriented, Situationally Aware, Working in Exception to Policy, Calculated Risk Takers, Strong Delegators, Great Listeners, Humble, and Change Agents, you've seen that a Fox is very much an entrepreneur. Foxes are strong leaders embracing innovation with initiative and thoughtfulness. These are the qualities that support effective culture change and the vigilant protection of healthy cultures. In the next chapter, you'll hear from Charlie Kirk as he talks about Turning Point USA and its efforts to change college culture, which not only impacts students' lives, but also reflects a shift in the college political landscape with new accountability to students.

6

Culture and Caring

"College isn't the place to go for ideas."—Helen Keller

A new and emerging trend is underway in academia where the closed structure of many colleges may not be so closed in the future. We're seeing the early signs of a power shift away from college leadership and tenured professors to students and the companies that ultimately will be hiring them, particularly given the introduction of online teaching to support social distancing, which could mean fewer professors in the future. More and more students (and their parents) are becoming aware that they have not been getting what they've been asked to pay for—a well-rounded and diverse education—as evidenced by student enrollment being in its eighth year of decline in 2019.

Not to say that this is happening everywhere, but many young adults who ultimately want to enter the workforce don't want to spend huge sums of money to be programmed in one-sided radicalism and, as such, are looking for alternatives. On a small but growing number of campuses today, students are starting to be educated with diversity of thought to understand what socialism and capitalism actually are and what they are not. At the same time, this is happening in the current crisis and new distributed learning environment, which is exposing students to a form of socialism—one where the government determines when you can travel and where you can go, what beaches you can visit, and what you can and cannot do there. These and other restrictions are certainly appropriate to controlling the spread of the virus, but they also model an aspect of socialism that can be eye opening.

Some students are choosing to take a gap year and learn a bit about real life and save up for tuition, or go into the trades or a junior college. Whatever the alternative, the variety of options is bringing power to the students in their vote to attend or not attend certain colleges. And while many colleges run with little accountability, as a closed structure, the continued decline in student enrollment cannot be ignored. Adding to this student power shift is the support of companies that recognize that colleges today are not turning out productive workers and leaders who will support company structure and healthy culture. Look to the United Kingdom as an example. Is the chaos in current British leadership and the Brexit failure due to the people in political office, or does it lie deeper—with the colleges that educated them? As of December 2019, twenty-eight British prime ministers have attended the University of Oxford and fourteen went to the University of Cambridge.[1]

The Power Base within colleges is shifting, perhaps giving way to the new and open gig culture. And at the forefront of this trend is Turning Point USA.

---

1   www.blanchflower.org/alumni/pm.html

Turning Point USA[2] is an organization that is in a unique position to observe academic culture within our colleges today and relate it to the corporate world, particularly its impact on company culture. Heading up Turning Point and providing this perspective is Charlie Kirk, a young man who personifies biblical leadership with clarity of thought, vision, compassion, conviction, and courage. These traits also characterize the culture at Turning Point, a team dedicated to building future leaders for America. Charlie Kirk says:

If we view academic culture as a living, breathing organism and conceptually drop it into a company today that has built and supports a Client-Centric Culture, which is also considered a living entity, the one will destroy the other. Certainly there are exceptions, but like it or not, the college system in many countries is one that imbues kids with egalitarian philosophy. It's the belief that all people should have equal rights from birth; political, economic, and social equality. And in an academic setting that works for most students. It sounds fair and it sounds good, as there is little structure in their lives during those days. But in a company, structure and hierarchy, along with the culture that supports them, are critical to leadership, stability, and organizational performance. But that's not equality. Now, fast forward to interviewing a recent graduate for a position within a company, and something else surfaces. In many colleges, egalitarian views are tightly coupled with Marxism, which has at its socioeconomic core a focus on social transformation and conflict. That is to say that it's not enough to

---

2   TPUSA is a 501(c)3 non-profit organization whose mission is to identify, educate, train, and organize students to promote freedom.

want equality, you need to fight for it. So, you're an executive in a growing company with a healthy culture and you're getting ready to interview a college graduate.

The resume looks great, as they all do, and you're expecting the individual to know a bit about your company. After all, the website does a pretty good job describing the business, the value it provides customers, and the firm's corporate vision, direction, priorities, and more. You might also wonder how much the candidate will know about you, as you're active on LinkedIn. Then comes the interview, but the person is late. Okay, you get past that and through the pleasantries to look into his eyes, only to see a blank stare. Well, okay again, and you begin to talk about the company and role when soon you're interrupted. The candidate wants to know about your diversity policy and how it's reflected in the company's culture. You answer and get back on tract. But he's not finished with his questions, as he expresses interest in a manage-ment position, while discounting the need for the core competencies and experience required for the job. Fortunately, there are graduates who will support your hiring protocols and company culture out there, and you look forward to talking with them. But for now, the experience has been fatiguing and unproductive.

This scene doesn't reflect the majority of graduates, but it's a number that's growing. And when it does happen, it's a near total disconnect that exists because you're speaking at cross purposes. Your focus is on the role, responsibilities, and business value that it represents to the firm, along with assessing the candidate's ability to do the job. His focus is on assessing the corporate environment and the opportunity to change it to be more aligned with the academic culture that he idealistically believes in and is prepared to defend by driving change in your company. Again, there will be exceptions, particularly with Turning Point Chapter students, but for many companies it's a troubling trend. That said, the candidate's desired change can be described on a continuum from being disruptive to corporate culture, to burning it down as an arsonist—the latter capturing the veracity of some graduates' beliefs. *The problem is that many companies, ever-so-well intentioned, are not proactively recognizing the downside of hiring graduates with a belief system that is counter to their company's good and healthy culture.* This suggests two lines of thought:

- The first is to integrate culture screening into your hiring process. This is not to judge, but to assess what a person believes to be important in the work environment, which can be determined with behaviorally based structured interviews. These interviews situationally focus on:

  ○ Beliefs – Something that you confidently trust to be true
  ○ Values – Something's level of importance to you
  ○ Morals – Behavior that you hold to be right or wrong
  ○ Ethics – Behavior that is generally viewed as acceptable based upon universal fairness.

The goal is to better understand if an individual will likely fit in and contribute to strengthening the existing good company culture or help transform a bad culture into a good one. To achieve as much objectivity as possible and to attain consistency, it's recommended that the major norms of existing culture be codified as a baseline. This can be accomplished by characterizing a part of the company that best illustrates the existing or desired culture. It may be a department, division, or business unit that then becomes the culture baseline and perhaps eventually the archetype for the entire organization.

- Culture screening cannot only be applied to the new hire interviewing process, but also to existing employees to help clarify what is expected of them and to assist them in that regard. Sometimes achieving better culture alignment is simply a matter of creating awareness and understanding with situational examples that illustrate the value and importance of working within the culture. It's making the intangible tangible for people, perhaps as a new work context that's centered on the best ways to get things done in the company.

Even with good culture screening, it only takes one bad apple to poison the environment in a company department; just one to begin changing corporate culture to the negative. In our view at Turning Point, when new college graduates hit around 5 percent of the workforce, critical mass has been reached to produce an activist movement that's hard to control: one that believes that feelings are more important than objective truth and facts. And that leads to chaos, as authority and leadership supported by the company competency-based hierarchy is deconstructed. While it's rare that any company would allow this to fully develop, the effort to contain it is one that sucks the oxygen out of the air for others, including managers who find themselves responsible for high maintenance employees. This is why culture screening at the initial phase of new hire interviewing is so important. Not just for college graduates, but for all new hires. Will they contribute to the norms and expectations of your functioning and healthy culture? Or, will they want to tear it down? *In today's world, good company culture requires vigilant protection.*

"You can't have a value structure without a hierarchy. They're the same thing because a value structure means one thing takes precedence over another," says Jordan Peterson. Leadership, performance, and organizational stability are dependent on the value structure that hierarchy represents and, again, that is counter to equality. Try to mix the two and the emulsion will spell disaster, expressed as management and operational chaos. That said, if an activist does get through initial screening, it's been our experience that deprogramming can take place and be effective within sixty days if the individual is provided with good direction and support. This requires a limited but strict rule set that, like the Ten Commandments, are expressed in the negative.

For example, you can tell a graduate new hire to be courteous when in meetings, which is a positive rule expression. The inverse consists of negative rules that are explicitly clear. Such as, do not use your phone when in meetings and do not be late to meetings. This is important as graduates can easily define "courteous" to be whatever they want it to be based upon their indoctrination in college. It's an issue of precise clarity and accountability. Again, there will always be student exceptions and schools that do not negatively inculcate students, like Liberty University. Liberty, a private evangelical Christian university in Lynchburg, Virginia, builds leaders in the spirit of serving others through creativity and a passion for wisdom, and does so in the name of Christ. And when we refer to "wisdom," we don't mean wisdom from society, but rather wisdom from knowledge where the true source of that knowledge is the Bible. Like Tuning Point, this is an organization that does not view the Bible as a collection of mythical fables, as much of academia would have students believe. But unlike Liberty, Turning Point is indirectly enabling college students to read between the lines. They see and hear Turning Point present new and independent thinking that reflects diversity of thought based upon strong values. And they wonder, from where does all this come? What is the source of the wisdom and strength that Turning Point demonstrates every day? And so, they ask. And our response is to point to Christ. This is significant because it reflects inductive reasoning and a desire to get to the source of truth. With a little help, young adults are figuring it out themselves. And it is our hope that companies will, as well. After all, how can a company build a strong healthy culture and not know the real source of truth?

As mentioned, most colleges are closed environments, projecting an image of insulation that can cause company leaders to believe that the colleges cannot be influenced. In science, we refer to this as a closed system with inputs and outputs. However, the inputs to academic culture and its indoctrination of students can be influenced, and outputs can be filtered. Turning Point is now influencing students in high school, starting early to build independent thinking leaders that have the benefit of family support, and hopefully attending a school that is centered on learning with discipline and hard work. Companies can do the same, reaching out to younger people—going deeper into the supply chain for future talent. Think of it as a river flowing from high school to college to the workforce. If that river gets polluted, it affects everything downstream and into the lake of employment. So ideally, you educate against pollution in high school, filter out pollution post-college with good culture screening, and provide a clear blue stream of water to nourish the growth of companies and individual careers throughout society.

Charlie's river metaphor is an important one in that pointing high school kids in the right direction and selecting the right college could shape the trajectory of their lives. And sometimes that direction can point to a junior college. When I was in high school, I really didn't have the motivation or ability to learn. If I didn't make any trouble for the teachers and tried to apply myself somewhat, I would get Cs. That said, when graduation time came around something happened. By the grace of God, I woke up and decided that I wanted to go to engineering school. Given my track record, it was an insane ambition. Fortunately, I didn't know that. But there was another problem. I had skipped gym my entire senior year, as the school had computerized class administration and left me off the gym schedule. Thankfully, I had been on the gymnastics team and the coach applied that to the gym requirement.

With that, the next challenge was getting into an engineering college. I applied everywhere but did poorly on the SATs. Not surprisingly, everywhere I applied, I was turned down. Then, I came upon Massachusetts Bay Community College that had just announced a one-year engineering transfer program. The idea was that if you were successful at Mass Bay, you could then transfer to a four-year college with one year of credit. But for this to work, the program had to be highly credentialed with very challenging first-year engineering courses.

So, I applied and went in for an interview. It was like any other interview with all the right questions yet followed by all the wrong answers on my part. So, you can imagine my surprise when the gentleman said, "We're going to accept you," which was quickly followed by, "but you won't make it. The only reason we are letting you in is because we have twenty-nine students enrolled and we need thirty for state funding."

For some reason his negative prediction didn't faze me, and while not encouraging, I was in. Classes included courses like inorganic chemistry, physics, calculus, and analytical geometry. Within a week I knew that I was dead in the water. I might as well have been on planet Mars, as I was not even close to comprehending any of the subjects. But God then put a notion into my head that reflected wisdom that I certainly did not have. I went to the Hilltop Steakhouse on Route 1 in Saugus, my hometown. I had gone to high school with the owner's son and asked for a job to work weekends. For two days a week I worked nonstop in the kitchen. Then, I took that money and went to MIT to hire the smartest senior I could find. His name was Stan and to this day, I wonder if he was an angel. He worked with me two nights a week, helping me with my homework and teaching me how to learn. At the end of the first semester, 50 percent of the class flunked out, but

I survived. During the second semester, somehow, I shifted into high gear doing stuff like Millikan's Oil Drop experiment in physics, which was a second-year experiment at MIT. At the end of the program I was the only one to go on to engineering school. Northeastern University accepted me as sophomore to pursue my BSEE degree.

The bridge from high school to college is one of the most important times in a person's life. And Turning Point is there. Charlie is there. And my Charlie was Stan.

Caring, Culture, and Science

Newton's Third Law speaks to conservation of momentum. That is, for every action there is an equal and opposite reaction in nature. You're looking at a pond where a beaver is sitting on a log. Suddenly, he jumps off. He moves in one direction and the log moves in the other direction. The beaver moves several feet, but the log moves only an inch. This is because the momentum of the log must equal the momentum of the beaver. His mass is small, so his velocity is higher than that of the log that has lots of mass but moves very slowly. As momentum is mass times velocity, the mass times the velocity of the beaver must equal the mass times the velocity of the log. The two equal and opposite momentum vectors cancel out, meaning that there is only so much momentum and that if one has it, the other does not.

Now, apply this to sales. In a competitive sales situation, if your sales momentum increases, it must be at the direct expense of the competition's sales momentum. We know this because we can quantify sales momentum, which again equals mass times velocity. Here, mass is your support base that is measured by looking at the level of political power your contacts have. Are they Foxes? Inside the Power Base or outside the Power Base? This combined with the nature of your relationship with them will determine your level of customer support or mass, where relationship is measured in terms of Ally, Supporter, Neutral, or Opponent. Combine this with the rate at which you're building competitive advantage, also measurable, and you have the level of sales momentum. Momentum means inertia, which is the resistance of an object in motion to change direction or speed. In sales, this is critical.

Stuff happens: a client reorganization; a new competitor emerges; or perhaps a buy, sell, or merger. Whatever it is, change is inevitable and when it occurs, it's your sales momentum that helps protect your sales campaign from being derailed. When a client down select occurs, the top few suppliers with the most sales momentum are chosen. When a supplier decision is made, it's because the sales momentum of one supplier exceeds the sum of their competitor's sales momentum at the decision point in time. Again, conservation of momentum dictates that when your sales momentum increases, it must be at the direct expense of the competition. Sometimes this is based upon the value you provided to the client and good selling, but it can also be because your competition made a mistake in their sales campaign. At that very point, the competitor's sales momentum is transferred to you.

It is this type of STEM thinking that drives our AI algorithms for sales forecasting vs. traditional machine learning methods. And just as these math models produce accurate predictions of sales outcomes early in time, this type of thinking will also provide you with key insights that the competition will likely not have, giving you a nontraditional source of competitive advantage to build sales momentum. But what conceptually sits behind this thinking is caring about the customer.

The Science of Caring

Let's look at culture where CX or Customer Experience is driven by the level of caring for customers and also apply it to employees within a company. Here, caring momentum is also subject to the law of conservation of momentum, as there is only so much of it available within an organization—and within an individual. When you think about it, how many family members and close friends can you really care about, in terms of mindshare, spending time with, and supporting? What happens when you make a new close friend? Can you maintain the same level of caring for everyone?

Brunello Cucinelli is an Italian designer and CEO of his luxury wear company located in the village of Solomeo. With 20 percent of his profits going to charity—like restoring the medieval church in his village—Cucinelli places a significant emphasis on his community and employees. They work in a beautiful environment with one wall comprised of all windows looking out to a picturesque landscape. Employees enjoy a ninety-minute provided lunch in the dining room and are required to work no later than 5:30 p.m., as Cucinelli believes that working too many hours will "steal your soul." This is a company that really values its staff. But if you go to the company's store you will find it to be like an outlet here in the United States. There are no service people other than a cashier. Caring for employees is through the roof, but caring for customers is noticeably absent. In this example, the staff are the metaphorical log and the customers are the beaver.

Now, shift back to companies in America. Ideally, caring would be balanced between customers and employees, and in some companies, it is. But in firms with Looking Glass Cultures, caring is not there for clients. And when sellers are viewed as the problem or the cause of declining sales effectiveness, caring is not with employees either. So, who is the caring centered on? In our view, the caring is focused on the senior leadership of the company.

They are the ones the company culture cares the most about, which helps to explain the incredible resilience of a Looking Glass Culture and its ability to discount customers and employees when company and sales practices simply don't make sense. The irrational becomes rational to them and because of their power, it goes unchallenged. The company's board of directors is configured by the CEO with specifically chosen people who are well compensated. Similarly, the senior executive staff is handpicked and well incentivized to support the CEO. The internal checks and balances are in name only, subject only to the will of the CXO executives. Certainly, this is not the case everywhere, as Looking Glass Cultures are not everywhere, but they are prominent and growing in number across America.

Caring in any company culture will appear to have its center of gravity somewhere among customers, employees, or senior management. In the physical world, this is the point at which the entire weight of something can be balanced. Here, the balance refers to the place in an organization that can direct where the caring is focused: to customers, employees, and/or executive leadership. When it comes to setting a company's business direction and priorities, this place is at corporate executive leadership; the CXO level. But when it comes to culture there is a subtlety involved. Yes, culture and caring are definitely influenced by the top people in an organization, but those are actually shaped, directed, and maintained by key Foxes in the influential collective—that is, very powerful and well-connected Foxes who can exist throughout the organization. *When it comes to culture, the center of gravity is where you would least expect it, and that is one of the reasons that culture is so elusive and challenging to manage.*

It is one of the rare examples where physics does not apply; like the distribution of sellers producing the most revenue where a Gaussian distribution or bell curve should apply but doesn't. Rather the 80/20 rule often applies where 20 percent of the sellers produce 80 percent of the business. That's because sales performance is not a phenomenon of nature, but of people. And the same is true with culture and the focus of caring that it drives.

Today, in the corporate world, the balance of caring has largely been lost with the advent of the gig culture that has given rise to the Looking Glass Culture. Providing customers with significant business value—differentiated from that of the competition, through the good work of talented and motivated employees—is no longer the real priority. So, what's the problem? Do people not care anymore? No, they care; but it's who and what they care about that's important. *At the core of a Looking Glass Culture is deception. And the key individuals who are at the epicenter of the influential collective are not actually Foxes; they are Jackals who, as mentioned earlier, look and talk like Foxes but aren't.*

They are individuals who are intelligent, personable, and able to see, understand, and capitalize on the trends of the gig culture and prevailing company growth strategies, but only to advance their own interests at the expense of the company, its clients, and employees:

The Looking Glass has a heart,
But is it a Fox?
Can't tell the Jackal apart,
Putting sellers in a box.

And how do they pull this off? By largely focusing the caring onto the people who keep them in power: the corporate executives. In too many companies, leadership gets the recognition, compensation, and the apparent "control" over business direction and priorities, while the Jackals get the power behind the scenes to advance their own agendas and ideology.

Summary of Chapter 6

In this chapter, you were introduced to what's really going on in colleges today and its impact on companies when hiring college graduates who have been indoctrinated with egalitarian and Marxist ideology. With an orientation of equality for all and the compelling need to transform companies away for their structure and hierarchy, companies can find themselves not hiring assets to the business, but rather liabilities. While there are exceptions, these student graduates don't recognize the need for structure to support leadership, stability, and organizational performance, which can seriously damage a productive and healthy company culture.

What sits behind any culture is a caring for people, which is viewed in this chapter as being of finite amount within people and organizations. This is a new concept backed by observation and science. As such, caring can be focused superficially across many people or applied in depth and with substance to a few people. In companies this focus can be on customers, employees, and/or senior management, as directed by the center of gravity for caring, which is a group of individuals who shape, direct, and maintain the caring focus.

They are the collective Foxes who really control company culture—that is, in healthy cultures, such as Client-Centric Cultures. In Looking Glass Cultures, they are not Foxes, but Jackals who create deception at the heart of such cultures. They direct a caring attitude toward senior management to maintain power through the association with high authority, but often at the expense of real productivity and customers. They are experts at managing up. That said, the moments of truth with clients can ever so subtly illuminate their presence.

What happens when the moments of truth, experienced by sellers in the pursuit of important deals, shine a light onto a Looking Glass Culture that has the potential to sabotage sales campaigns, yet the people who can most effectively intervene don't see what's happening? This is the focus of our next chapter.

7

When Seeing Is Not Believing

"Welcome out of the cave, my friend. It's a bit colder out here,
but the stars are just beautiful."—Plato

What happens when a seller experiences the moments of truth mentioned earlier, but doesn't see their significance? Busy work, distractions, and access to massive amounts of information make it difficult to see anything in today's gig culture and corporate world. But what's happening when sellers, sales managers, and senior executives *do* see the ill effects of a Looking Glass Culture and it simply doesn't register? The decline in sales effectiveness, lost deals, slow pipeline velocity with deals continually being pushed out, and on, are all visible, but not truly *seen*. Tell someone about the reality of political influence and they believe it; tell them that the paint is wet, and they need to touch it. Culture is the same: you need to touch it in the form of the moments of truth that signal a Looking Glass Culture. With the right focus and mindset, you can recognize what's happening. You can see the consequences of lost business clearly enough to know that something is wrong, even though the culture will attempt to normalize the irrational to a point where it appears rational.

Cultural Preoccupation

To explore this, let's look at a scenario in which a seller completed his MBA from an Ivy League school and moved to the West Coast to begin his career selling to semiconductor merchants. With a very strong focus on the client and a consultative approach, he proceeded to spend six months doing an analysis of the semiconductor fabrication (fab) process for a specific company. Let's assume that he was actually working to generate demand by discovering the potential to create an opportunity. His sales campaign was all about process improvement focused on a new silicon carbide substrate that was ideal for high power, high frequency devices.

The problem was that this material was in scarce supply and the semiconductor companies manufactured their devices in batch mode where there were many devices per substrate. If a problem existed in the fabrication process, all the devices on a particular substrate would be lost. Having come up with a solution for this, the seller built a proposal and began discussing it with the client. His observations were good, his facts were good, and his recommendations for higher yield improvement were good. What wasn't good was that he had gone native.

That is, he became so intensely focused on the client and their business that he felt he was working for them and not his own company. He took empathy for the client to an extreme, which is the opposite of what we most often see in gig culture, yet it was still a problem. His sales manager pointed out that he was likely not aligned with the right client individuals. While his process improvement recommendations were aligned with client corporate priorities, he was not talking to the stakeholders for those priorities or aligned with the Power Base, and that was slowing down client responsiveness.

Still, there was another problem. He had talked to enough of the wrong people that the competition soon got wind of what was happening and were savvy enough to get hold of his recommendations. Aligned with senior management and the Power Base, they repackaged and refined his solution to provide even more business value, while also advancing the personal motivators of key client executives. The result was a loss not only of the sale that carried a high business development expense, but also of the seller's credibility within his company. So, what really went wrong?

The seller, with all good intentions, became fixated or preoccupied not just with the client, but with the fabrication process improvement opportunity. This preoccupation with his solution—like the gig culture characteristic of being preoccupied with product or service that can depersonalize a loss—created an attitude of self-deception supported by defensiveness. The self-deception manifested itself in rationalizing away the relevance and importance of what the seller's sales manager was trying to get across to him. He had put all his faith in the solution and could not see beyond it. And when the sales manager pushed harder to convince him to align with the right client executives, while he had strong competitive differentiation, a defense mechanism kicked in to reduce the anxiety of having to believe that his solution would not carry the day. This is an unconscious psychological defensiveness that arises from an unacceptable or potentially harmful stimuli. And that stimuli was the sales manager.

Listening to him and altering the sales approach was perceived to be riskier than staying true to believing totally in the solution. And while this was going on, every minute he spent selling to the wrong client individuals, his vulnerability to a "do nothing" client decision or a competitive threat went up with the square of time. The three weeks of meetings with the wrong people increased his competitive vulnerability and exposure by a factor of nine. It was a colossal setback in his sales campaign at exactly the wrong time when the sales situation was peaking.

In our example, the seller had put his faith in the solution to the point where his preoccupation and strong belief in the solution created a kind of tunnel vision and thinking. It became something to protect. It is the same with a product-centric sales culture and the inward focus that drives one-to-many generic solutions and an insensitivity to clients. Individuals put their faith in what is perceived to be expected internal behavior to the point of fixation or preoccupation that kills their ability to see reason, to see the moments of truth even when put directly in front of them.

We were recently in a meeting with a pursuit team that was service-offering obsessed with an important opportunity. When our team spoke up and explained that the number one shareholder of the client had stated that the company would buy, sell, or merge with another company it fell on deaf ears. This shareholder was known for turning around businesses successfully and had been constantly increasing his share position in the client company to the point of having enough ownership to have multiple seats on the board and the ability to call a shareholder's meeting whenever he wanted. He was clearly the corporate executive Fox running the show from behind the CXO team. But culture and service-offering preoccupation, along with an inward focus, created an attitude of self-deception supported by defensiveness, as the moments of truth passed by, one by one, until finally the sales campaign was derailed by the wrong solution focus that was not short-term accretive to shareholders in a buy, sell, or merge situation.

The Culture Paradox

Within culture there is a paradox. In a company the bureaucracy is again part of the culture—created out of the culture. Therefore, the bureaucracy cannot change culture. It is also true that cultural inhabitants whose behavior is dictated by the culture cannot easily change the culture. It takes some level of detachment to break the paradox; that speaks to sellers who have one foot in and one foot out of the culture—that is one foot in the company and one foot in client organizations.

Not long ago, a company that is an industry leader hired us to help them understand why they had not been able to grow for two years. As part of our investigation, we spoke to a large transportation company that had decided not to go with our client and to instead purchase a solution from a smaller and unproven competitor. Speaking with the customer's executives we realized that a number of moments of truth had presented themselves. We were told:

- The supplier did not listen; we asked for blue and got green;
- The supplier's focus was on locking us into a license and not addressing our needs. Everything they said was pretext;

- The supplier constantly pressured us to bend and comply with their views, sales goals, and timelines;
- The supplier advised us to operate in exception to our beliefs and culture.

The result was to create a perception of arrogance and insensitivity to the business needs of the customer. When we asked the company how they were doing with the competitor, the response was, "We don't know if they will be successful. We just know that we could not go forward with the incumbent."

When we came onto the scene the account executive had already been fired—an all-too-often solution that can be symptomatic of a much more fundamental cultural problem. This is not to say that believing in your company and solutions is not important. For sure that's critical. But what is also critical is not crossing the line between believing in your company and developing a preoccupation with a Looking Glass Culture that creates an arrogance protected by self-deception driven by defensiveness. At the heart of this defensiveness is usually fear.

Psychologists tell us that internalized fear, regret, or guilt are things that people can easily begin to ruminate or become fixated on; reflecting on something over and over again. When that happens, a person's imagination can kick in, creating images of a worst-case situation.

For example, say you're working in a counterculture manner, not following accepted cultural norms, in order to secure an important piece of business. That is, the sales campaign requires you to propose X, but a powerful person in your company wants you to propose Y because it's important to your company's growth plan. Also assume that going against the wishes of the executive could potentially put your job at risk and going against what the customer needs and expects could put the deal at risk. And so, you begin to imagine all the bad things that could happen by not following the executive directive; professionally, economically, and at home, if you lose your position. *As the brain and unconscious mind has no ability to differentiate between imagination and reality,[1] perceived risk develops into fear and then physiologically into anxiety.*

When that anxiety gets too high and surpasses the fear of losing a deal, you think twice about proposing X. After all, clients will come and go, but you will continue to live with the people in your company, people who can advance or inhibit your career. Is the risk of a sales loss greater than that of a career loss? Particularly when you're supporting a powerful executive who can protect your back politically from the loss? In a gig culture where individual security is diminishing, going along to get along internally becomes an easy choice for many people. You're labeled a team player by the executive; perceived risk, fear, and anxiety decrease, making it easy to rationalize proposing Y. For example, you say to yourself, "The client doesn't really know what they need, so I should challenge them on the approach of X vs. Y." This opens the door to irrational logic, viewing the client as incompetent and saving your company from bad business.

The preoccupation and internalization of a Looking Glass Culture will, as we have said, produce an inward focus, while also desensitizing many sellers to client needs. But in some cases, you'll see a phenomenon where a seller completely believes that what the culture

---

1   Reference: drdavidhamilton.com/does-your-brain-distinguish-real-from-imaginary/

dictates is *the* way and *the only way* of getting things done. The individual may not like it, but believes that "it is what it is, and we have to live with it." It's this type of thinking that takes us back to before the four-minute mile was broken by runners. At that time, everyone believed that it wasn't possible. Then, one day it was broken, which was immediately followed by several runners breaking it. The mindset that it was not possible was strong enough to discourage runners from trying. And so it is with culture.

Some people absolutely believe that the culture must be followed because it cannot be changed. And to work in exception to it is to perhaps be disloyal to the company, or maybe to go against the wishes of senior management, which might have career implications. Whatever the reason, they believe that the "four-minute culture" cannot be broken. In our example of the monkeys and how they protect the culture, it simply would not occur to one of them to assist the new monkey in climbing to the top of the rocks for the banana and guide him to the other side of the rock pile to perhaps have protection from the spray of water and to enjoy half of the banana.

Have you ever tried to reason with a person of strong opposite beliefs? An individual who, for example, believes with heart and soul in some radical political, religious, philosophical, or other type of theory? What has been your experience? Were you able to bring logic and reality into the picture in an effective way? Does any form of deductive reasoning prevail? Not often. Some people tune out when you try to get them to see from another point of view, others become angry and walk away, while still others go on the attack and accuse you of being some sort of radical or racist yourself.

"When the debate is lost, slander becomes the tool of the loser," said Socrates. This inability to participate in constructive dialogue stems from the same interpersonal phenomenon that we've been talking about with culture. Confronted with the most sensitive and constructive intent, any person with radical beliefs—whether they stem from cultural preoccupation or something else—will often coil up like a snake, shift into a protective mode to reduce the anxiety of having to accept the truth, and self-protect with a defensive mindset. But thankfully, not all people are that way. The Bible in Matthew 23:12 says, "And whosoever shall exalt himself shall be abased; and he that shall humble himself shall be exalted." Humility is the gateway to insight and wisdom.

As we saw in the words spoken by Satya Nadella, CEO of Microsoft, and in the acknowledgement by now President Trump when he made it clear that he knew nothing about how to fix a broken ice-skating rink, humility is the cornerstone of leadership and entrepreneurialism. It is also the essence of freedom, in terms of being open minded and free of intellectual and emotional restraint. Freedom to do the right thing and freedom that supports diversity of thought result from humility. Yes, these freedoms will be put to the test when confronted by radical anything, whether it be a Looking Glass Culture or anything else that is out of touch with reality. As such, humility is one of the most important defining traits of an effective seller whose aim is to win business and improve sales culture.

Humility and the Cultural Change Agent

The need for humility not only applies to cultural inhabitants who are trying to manage and deal with people stricken with radical beliefs and cultural preoccupation, but also to the people whom the seller, sales manager, or executive is trying to recruit as part of the cultural Power Base to drive cultural change. Individuals radicalized by a culture will often be devoid of humility and receptivity, treating the needed changes with contempt, characterized by derision and disbelief. It's an attitudinal state of mind that can extend beyond cultural changes, themselves, and often be applied to the people who create and defend the narrative for change.

In other words, if you work to improve a Looking Glass Culture, expect to be assertively challenged. Therefore, it's very important to avoid such culturally cemented people, particularly the Jackals, before you build your support base for change. "Do not rebuke a mocker or he will hate you; rebuke a wise man and he will love you" (Proverbs 9:8). It may not be possible to avoid engaging with these people but be aware that it puts you in the crosshairs and underscores the need to quickly get to the right Fox—a Fox who demonstrates the following core traits by his or her actions:

- Change Agent, with good situational awareness of what's going on with company culture;
- Powerful, and respected for achieving results;
- Humble, with the ability to listen;
- Trustworthy, clearly different from that of a Jackal. This is the most important trait. If you trust the wrong powerful person, all hope of real success can be lost.

No cultural change initiative will succeed without the right Fox at the helm with you early on. That said, the support of the *right* Fox is a requirement in any challenging situation—a lesson I learned early in life, albeit in a different context.

When I was a kid, I had the misfortune to attend a not-so-nice Catholic school whose culture in teaching kids was based upon inducing fear and strict obedience by inculcating us with unbiblical principles coupled with abuse. It was the most destructive environment anyone could imagine. Physiologically, it was as effective as a North Korean prisoner of war camp where I understand captives were stripped of all self-worth to the point where no one even attempted to escape. As such, there were no fences, no barbed wire, no guards on duty. They simply were not required due to the psychological programming that occurred every day. While my school was on the East Coast, it might as well have been in North Korea.

Finally, in an effort to survive, I told my dad about what was happening. He was a retired Navy pilot on the Yorktown CV-5 during WWII, flying with a torpedo squadron. Known as a Mustang, he was a commissioned officer who began his career as an enlisted service member prior to commissioning. And on top of that, he was a boxer on the ship. I say this not to brag on my father, but to make the point that if anyone could help me in my situation, I believed it to be him—he was my Fox. He then came with me to school and spoke with the nuns who unfortunately lied and misled him. But it was not really the nuns who lied; it was the culture of the organization that lied. My parents simply could not believe that such lies were possible in the church. Similar to our cultural examples earlier, the anxiety of even just considering that the nuns or priests would lie was so great that self-deception set in quickly. Their self-deception brought them to only one possible conclusion: I was the one lying.

At that point, I was alone, just like a seller sitting at the cross-roads of doing something that's required for a client or being true to a Looking Glass Culture. Like that seller, I was truly alone with no one to help me. The next morning, I boarded the bus to school. When I arrived at the school, however, I went across the street into a drug store, gave the attendant my dime to use the pay phone (as I could not reach it), and called home. Speaking to my mom, I refused to go into the school. If she insisted I do so, I was prepared to run away, like a seller perhaps deciding that enough is enough. But that didn't happen, as she told me to come home and I was later put in a fifth grade public school class.

What my parents didn't know was the nature and extent of the destructive cultural programming of that Catholic school and the impact it had on me. For example, one day in public school, I observed a boy swinging his legs while sitting and quickly went over to him to explain that he was "giving the devil a ride," and to stop it. For me, it was an act of kindness, trying to help him. For others, it was an act of insanity. My programming was so effective that I could not adequately partic-ipate in any social environment and was, once again, alone. But this time I didn't even try to seek help from my parents as I believed it was me who was flawed, yet not knowing why. Being "dysfunctional," the school kept me back in the fifth grade for another year believing that I was somehow mentally disabled (but expressed in not-so kind words).

At that point all self-worth was gone and I was left with muddling my way forward as best I could. It took me years, until I was a senior in high school, to figure things out by the grace of God and find a way into college. That said, I didn't really know the difference between religion and Christianity. For me it was all the same and I despised it. Every time I came upon a priest at the airport, in public, or on a plane where I had him captive, I would challenge his religion with surgical precision and assertiveness, recounting my experience and insisting he defend his faith in that which hurt so many kids.

It wasn't until much later that I began to understand that religion is man's interpretation of God, as compared to Christianity, which is God's revelation to man. For me, it meant humbling myself and giving up the anger at my past mistreatment, in order to accept divine support and make the transition from victim to survivor where it was no longer necessary to hate the ones who had caused me so much grief in my life. That was possible through my newfound ability to forgive and to understand, "… but with humility comes wisdom" (Proverbs 11:2).

The qualities of change agent, power, and humility were not my own, but they were with me. Prior to that I was into retribution; punishment being inflicted on priests as vengeance for the wrongdoing I'd received. But that's all behind me and who would have known that my crazy experience as a kid would help to equip me to recognize and understand how culture is damaging people and sales effectiveness in today's professional world.

Summary of Chapter 7

In this chapter, you saw the danger of being preoccupied and fixated on a Looking Glass Culture that is blind to the moments of truth that originate with clients and signal that something is wrong. It's then that clients are discounted, not listened to, and subjugated to what's best for the supplier. As this destructive culture has, by definition of its very existence, been internalized and supported by powerful people, the response to challenging it will be quick and aggressive. This makes it very easy for sellers to play it safe and not jeopardize their careers for the sake of a deal. Fear and anxiety from within are always more powerful than those of losing a deal to a competitor or getting no decision from the client.

In the next chapter, you'll be able to broaden your view of culture with unconventional thinking that will deepen your understanding of it. Earlier, Charlie Kirk introduced the concept of looking at culture as you would a person or organism. In our next chapter you'll gain new insight and see the personification of culture fully developed, via a unique approach that reveals certain qualities not generally seen by most people, yet absolutely necessary if you want to fully comprehend the company culture you are in.

8

Putting a Face on Culture

"Vision is the art of seeing what is invisible to others."—Jonathan Swift

Sellers are in the unique position of being able to see the mirror reflection of their sales and company culture through the eyes of their customers. If they are not blinded by their company's culture, they can understand the impact it has more than anyone else—including upper management—because they see it and live it in the field. Still, it's all too easy to ignore the power of culture or view it as abstract and think of it simply as an inanimate collection of values and norms that influence behavior in a particular environment. It might also be viewed as a set of attitudes, beliefs, and customs. All of these characterizations would be true, but at the same time they are so nondescript and intangible that they fall short of providing any real insight into how culture actually works, what drives it, what threatens it, and how it protects itself.

Few people think about these questions because the general view is to look at culture as some kind of invisible environment made up of transparent intellectual and behavioral rules. But it is not that at all.

Culture can rationalize and put emotion ahead of logic, as it tends to be resilient and fixed in its ways. Yet it can also be kinetically dynamic in fighting for what it wants and can proactively perceive threats and prepare to react to them with conviction and boldness. In short, we're not really talking about a thing or an it. For all intents and purposes, we're looking at a life form. Morphologically different from people, it behaves with human-like characteristics. This is the personification of culture.

Personifying Culture

Cultures are made up of people, with each culture consisting of a unique matrix of human qualities that are interdependent and inter-related in such a way as to form a "living" entity, one that can exert influence, for one purpose: to shape human behavior in very specific ways and to do so with scale. Why do we care about understanding the nature of this influence on people and behavior? To manage culture, we need to know it—intimately, know it. To not do so is to underes-timate its power to drive or resist change, which can manifest itself by dramatically slowing down or stopping needed cultural change. It's then that its abstract nature and the exertion of strong influence become very visible and very real.

To see culture is to know it. More specifically, to see it as a person, an intelligent life form, is to know it. Personification of a sophisticated entity—like culture that is made up of its cultural inhabitants—drives a more holistic view, including all of its human-like characteristics, and does so with observable depth. That makes culture "someone" that can draw power from very specific sources and use it to adapt and protect itself for good or for bad. Go against it and you will most likely become frustrated and fail or leave. That said, it's not invincible if you think outside the box and don't take it on directly with the traditional methods of legislation, policy, and even compensation.

The goal is not to destroy it, but to change it to be more aligned with what the company needs to be successful. All cultures resist change, as members hold on to legacy values and ways of doing things that carry significant momentum and inertia that resist change. So, what does culture look like as a "person," and how do we deal with it?

First of all, culture has strength and endurance. When a culture is formed, it reflects the values and what is important to the founders of the business. As the founders have power, the culture has power. Over time, as more and more Power Base people become cultural drivers, it transitions itself to what is more like an institution. An institution operates on established laws, practices, or customs that can be objective and subjective, formal and informal. The formal policies of a company, together with its informal norms and values, make up the company's culture. But what is a law or a policy? It's whatever the group in power wants it to be. Policies are put in place by powerful executives to effectively run the company, while also complying, as an example, with government regulations that are put in place by powerful public officials.

Likewise, informal norms for getting things done within a company also originate with powerful people who reside in the cultural Power Base. So, where does a culture get its power? From two sources: the Foxes who inhabit it and time. A culture's power is as real as that of its Foxes who are at the center of the culture's influential collective.

The longer those cultural practices are in place, the more powerful and entrenched they become. As time passes, more people take on those practices, to the point that the practices become internalized.

Go against a cultural practice and you go against the Foxes. It becomes personal. Attempt to change the culture and you're trying to change the minds, opinions, and views of powerful people who have taken the culture's norms and expectations to heart. So, effecting change is all about knowledge, wisdom, and the right actions that will alter the views and feelings of the appropriate Foxes. Remember, these views and feelings have existed for some time and will not change easily.

Secondly, a culture is intelligent. Just as people are intelligent, so it is with culture, which suggests that culture has understanding, an ability to know why certain norms are important. As such, strong and credible logic is required to have any hope of effecting cultural change. This is particularly true when change is disruptive and the goal is not to slowly transition a culture from A to B, but to transform it with some sense of speed. As such, a culture may show how smart it is by putting forth an argument against change with a voice that is heard loud and clear. The voice of rationalization, as described earlier, reduces fear and anxiety by opposing change through the self-deception of its cultural inhabitants.

Third, culture is emotional. This speaks to the subjective nature of culture. Individuals may not believe in the desired change, or they may fear it. On the other hand, they may be excited about it and be very supportive. Emotion can easily influence or even overrule intellect and understanding. It can discount it, tune it out, or embrace it by adding amplified strength and conviction to understanding and logic. Solomon spoke of this when he wrote, "So that you incline your ear to wisdom and apply your heart to understanding" (Proverbs 2:2), "The wise in heart are called discerning" (Proverbs 16:21), and "The heart of the discerning acquires knowledge" (Proverbs 18:18).

This indicates that in seeking wisdom, both emotion and intellect are connected. To change culture requires both emotion and knowledge where emotion reflects attitude and knowledge consists of information and skill. Skill suggests an ability to know what information is important and what is just noise. It is about discerning *context*, the setting within which something is happening, in order to know what's real and what's just *pretext*—something that's true, but not the reason why an individual is taking a particular action. But above all, it's about developing a sense for cultural *subtext*.

Subtext is an intangible, underlying, and often distinct theme that conceptually sits behind what you're experiencing in a culture. In sales, it "whispers" to a seller, providing insight as to who's really winning the business, what's really important to a client, which client individuals have power and influence, and what needs to be done to win the business. In culture, subtext reads words and emotions to uncover motivations and causal factors, such as ego, fear, or insecurity, along with other motives or agendas like winning a power play or advancing an effort to accomplish something not to be spoken of in the open. Or, it could simply be a motivation to protect cultural norms, particularly if they don't make business sense. It is an undertone not overtly identified; not mentioned explicitly, but there as harmony between people and behaviors or as a collective defensive mindset.

Generally speaking, mindset refers to a mental attitude that determines how you will interpret and respond to situations. This is good when it comes to identifying a possible threat, but it's bad when it comes to dealing with that threat. Culture continually operates with a defensive mindset, and just like a person, it shifts that mindset to go on the offensive when necessary. When walking down the streets of Chicago or any city late at night, a defensive mindset will cause you to have good situational awareness to see and prepare for what could be an assault or difficult situation. But if that happens, there will be no room for defensiveness. Yes, you will defend yourself. And yes, you will use a minimum of force and take every advantage to first escape any danger. But to do any of that successfully you will need an offensive mindset. You will have to make the shift from defensive to offensive thinking—and do it without freezing in place, which happens to most people under duress as hormones dump into the bloodstream.

Culture will make this shift, as well, and like military-trained and experienced individuals, culture will not freeze. As we have said before, culture will attempt to purge or destroy what it can't assimilate. As the person on the streets of Chicago in our example, you will run to safety or fight if necessary. And, you will do it quickly, as every moment of delay, once engaged, will mean physical damage and a lower likelihood of being able to stop the damage. Culture, on the other hand will transition to the offense and attack without delay. It will not run and will not hesitate to address any threat. It will always be ready to move with excellent situational awareness as it maintains a vigilant defensive mindset to detect anything that could challenge its norms and legacy practices, that is, anything that the culture cannot transform or align with its values. The cultural destruction of perceived invasive thinking suggests isolation and the discrediting of any individual who is acting in a countercultural manner.

Purging implies creating fear and discouragement that will lead the culturally noncompliant person to leave or take another job. That's what you're dealing with when you go against culture. And it's not a far cry from the gig culture itself that seems to more and more often drive and promote self-interest to the point of dehumanizing others with verbal abuse whenever someone doesn't like what someone else is saying or doing. *That said, those who dehumanize others demonstrate animalistic behavior that by definition dehumanizes themselves.*

It's easy for some executives to dismiss the inward focus of a Looking Glass Culture and its dehumanizing effect on customers. Perhaps they just don't think or care about it. But if they did, it would become evident that it reflects destructive thinking that drives down sales effectiveness. And while client insensitivity can be rationalized away, the fact remains that dehumanizing anyone or any group, when carried to its logical conclusion and allowed to develop to its fullest extent in an unchecked environment, leads to genocide. The depiction of Jewish people as rats in Nazi Germany and that of the Tutsi population as cockroaches in Rwanda makes clear that being anywhere on this continuum from insensitivity to a group and discounting it, to viewing them as inferior, to villainizing them, to seeking their elimination, is simply evil. While losing business is nothing in comparison to the extreme, being insensitive to clients is attitudinal subtext in a Looking Glass Culture, making it very easy to then villainize sellers as the problem that is causing sales losses.

To the discerning person, subtext is realized through inductive reasoning that happens unconsciously. Think of it as inference or instinct. In the world of self-defense, this comes from effective and consistent training. In business, this comes from intellect and experience, which is different from deductive reasoning which is driven by principles of logic, such as a syllogism: Major Premise, Minor Premise, and Conclusion. Subtext uncovers that which is not intended to be seen. To sense it, you need to look for the signs of its existence and then trust your feelings.

In a Looking Glass Culture, when things are happening that don't make sense—as seen in the moments of truth discussed earlier—subtext is present. For example, it may be attitudinally a lack of willingness to listen to the client. Often, irrational decisions and actions do not want to see the light of day. Opposite this, is perhaps why Solomon, using the language of his day that people could understand, referred so many times to the word "heart" in Proverbs to connect emotion and attitude to help people better understand and manage difficult situations.

Neurologists tell us that emotions directly impact decision making and learning. Therefore, emotion drives logic, as apparently neurosurgeons can attest. But not all people have the ability to discern subtext. It takes good thinking and focus to illuminate underlying motives and causal factors. It also requires a conscience. Conscience distinguishes right from wrong with an inner feeling that acts as a "voice." It signals and guides people while creating subtext for future behavior.

Ignored, conscience can be silenced. Worse, it can evolve to produce false and distorted guidance that is actually able to promote wrongdoing: "In fact, both their minds and consciences are corrupted." (Titus 1:15). Corruption of the conscience develops over time with repeated wrongful behavior. It produces a dysfunctional conscience that when combined with emotional desire—let's say to force-close a deal this quarter against the interests of the customer—results in disinformation or faulty guidance that looks like a "green light" to the individual. Wisdom is lost, yet the individual may be very intelligent, very self-confident. But what sits behind those attributes may be a cold disposition and lack of empathy for the customer, and perhaps for sellers, who—when influenced by Jackals and others who mistakenly see green lights—align with the inward company focus and lack of customer centricity. This could potentially lead to a high human price.

Losing revenue from large deals is a serious problem, but when good people's careers and lives are hurt in the process, it's an indication that the personality of the company is turning dark with a Looking Glass Culture. Perhaps even worse is when sellers stand up for what is right in the eyes of the customer and apply commonsense to save a deal, only to have their careers damaged and the sale lost.

Solomon also applies personification to wisdom, perhaps to more fully characterize wisdom and its importance: "Blessed is the man who finds wisdom, the man who gains understanding, for she is more profitable than silver and yields better returns than gold" (Proverbs 3:13). "She" is wisdom. And more specifically, she is described as a "sister." "Say to wisdom, 'You are my sister,' and call understanding your kinsman" (Proverbs 7:4). This may well underscore the importance of personifying wisdom, as a family member, along with the emotional aspect of it, which is not to be discounted when seeking wisdom to drive cultural change through the personification of culture.

The personification of culture illuminates the qualities of strength, intelligence, and emotion, as a kind of living breathing life form. This is not a poetic device, as in an imaginative style of expression, but rather a practical presentation of what cultural change initiatives must deal with to be successful. To change culture will require that the right people within the organization have these same qualities of strength from political alignment; intelligence to see and understand the realities of culture; and the emotional attributes of conviction, tenacity, and boldness that reflect real passion and commitment. It all adds up to having the wisdom to know what to do, the will to choose it, and the power to make it endure, which when you think about it, is key to the success of any important and challenging initiative.

Looking beyond the business world there is another domain that is even more complex and significant, as nearly every family has been touched by it in one way or another. It centered on a challenge that required personification and a view into a problem that could only be approached by this type of applied personification thinking. The personification of cancer. And as you will see, it will help to develop even more insight into culture.

The Zuza Story

Zuza was a small black kitten left at the doorstep of a veterinarian when we adopted him. He was named after a silver back gorilla that I helped hand rear at Brookfield Zoo outside of Chicago. "Zuza" means "gift" in Swahili. When Zuza was two and a half years old, he was diagnosed with multiple myeloma, an aggressive form of blood cancer. At that point, his condition was critical, with his weakened little body struggling to stay alive. The textbook protocol for multiple myeloma in cats was to prescribe Prednisone, a steroid, and Melphalan, a chemo agent. But the problem was that we could not find any evidence that any cat had ever survived more than ninety days with this disease.

As the chemo kills lots of fast dividing cells, it takes out cancer cells, while also compromising the patient's immune system. But it doesn't kill all the cancer cells and this form of cancer is genetically heterogenic, meaning that its genetic diversity will likely include chemo-resistant cancer cells. The patient goes into remission for a while; then the resistant cells begin to multiply in the face of a weakened immune system. Zuza would then relapse, and cats often become refractory in that the cancer then becomes resistant to all treatment. Even if Zuza could withstand the chemo approach (that also damages the GI track, compromising appetite and nutrient absorption), there simply was no end game with a chemo approach to saving Zuza.

The battle to save a life was not with the cancer alone. It was also with the medical establishment and its culture. Zuza was young and while that facilitated the rapid onset of the cancer, it could also be part of the solution, as his immune system was strong—similar to what is the case today with the Covid-19 virus and its reduced impact on younger people. With the limited research I had done, I intuitively knew that building up his immune system to leverage his youth made the most sense. But that reflected nontraditional thinking and would challenge the best medical minds as to the efficacy of chemo that was based on extending life and not preserving it.

At the same time my emotions were running at full speed and oscillating up and down. I was experiencing guilt and fear. Then, one night when I was alone, I nearly gave in to the textbook solution that the veterinary oncologist had been driving. Zuza was on the floor, his fur shaved from the biopsy procedures to confirm the diagnosis, despondent, weak, and unable to even purr. That's when the fear and anxiety really settled in, as we were going against the norms of medical thinking, culture, and acceptability—against the view of the medical community. That view suggested that if we went the chemo route, we would have done everything we could, absolving us of guilt. But in the deepest recesses of my heart, I knew that if we did that I would be giving myself permission to let go of the responsibility for Zuza's survival. I knew that what I was considering was not what was best for Zuza, but rather what was best for me. Upon that realization, I threw the Melphalan into the trash, said a prayer, and fired up the computer.

The protocol strategy was to build up Zuza's immune system, while doing everything possible to slow down the cancer; to buy time, to keep him alive. The technical term was immunomodulation, just a theory at the time, but the problem was that I didn't know what I didn't know. Everything was new to me and, at that time I had no idea what caused the cancer. Physicians have a word for not knowing what causes a disease: idiopathic. It was a label that gave me no comfort. The truth was that no one really knew what caused multiple myeloma and no one knew how to cure it.

What I did know was that I had to better understand what cancer really is, not in traditional medical terms, but as an adversary. That meant, I needed to view it as an intelligent entity that could thoughtfully respond to changing circumstances and adapt to chemical attack by turning chemo agents into resources, so I could defeat the cancer's ability to avoid natural cell death that enabled it to become seemingly immortal for the life of the patient, while proliferating and damaging the patient's immune system by producing dysfunctional antibodies and suppressing appetite. *Personifying cancer, just as with company culture, showed it to be strategic, intelligent, and strong.*

That's why no single-pronged attack, like using a single chemo agent, could kill the cancer. And that's why no one person can change culture. One individual can initiate culture change, as a catalyst, and support ongoing change, but alone, no one can do all the heavy lifting. In both cases, dealing with culture and cancer require a systems-oriented approach. The systems approach creates a dynamic that produces disproportionate results that are exponentially greater than most people can imagine.

Strength in Numbers

Multiple myeloma is a cancer that forms in a type of white blood cell called a plasma cell. Referred to as myeloma cells, they can be spotted by the dysfunctional antibodies they produce. These antibodies consist of a specific protein structure that can be identified with sophisticated blood and urine tests. The myeloma cells proliferate, increasing their numbers, and invade the bone marrow. While in the bone marrow, they link up with bone marrow stromal cells. Together they create a system where they potentiate each other, dramatically accelerating the proliferation of myeloma cells that clog up the bone marrow and spread to other organs. This strength-in-numbers approach is conceptually not indifferent from what a culture does to build itself up.

A fundamental emotional need of humans is to live in fellowship with others; to herd, as anthropologists say, or to be in community where people have something in common. For that reason, a Client-Centric Culture or Looking Glass Culture will actively attract people who share its values and work to promote those people into positions of power, sometimes independent of their performance. In this regard, a bad culture becomes worse, while a good culture sustains itself. *It also means that the time required to damage a culture is short, while the time to repair it is long:*

> *Good or bad or not,*
> *Culture is strong.*
> *But time to damage is short,*
> *While time to heal is long.*

Cultures change when a critical mass of the right people in the right organizational places with the right levels of power exert their influence.

The Dynamic of Potentiation

The cancer dynamic created by the partnership between myeloma and bone marrow stromal cells not only drives rapid growth of the cancer, but also makes it immortal. The cancer cells defeat what's called apoptosis and are no longer subject to programmed cell death like every other cell in our bodies. This dynamic happens because the cancer is smart enough to know the importance and location of the bone marrow stromal cells. It knows that if it produces a very specific chemical, which the stromal cells have a receptor for (or desire, if you will), that the stromal cells will then produce a different chemical that the cancer thrives on and that is highly inflammatory, increasing myeloma cell proliferation. The result is the exponential growth and metastasis or spreading of the cancer.

In culture, the strength and longevity of its traditional norms is determined by the potentiation of people and time. This is based upon the number of culture-supporting Power Base inhabitants, the overall number of cultural inhabitants, and how long the cultural norms have been in place. When all three are present and growing individually, the result is much greater than the sum of the parts. Powerful inhabitants set the norms and, as influence flows out of the Power Base, those norms spread to other cultural inhabitants over time, where time also deepens the norms within people. One by one, the norms are internalized by the culture's inhabitants. Accelerating this, Foxes are also connecting with, or creating other Foxes who share the same norms.

The result is an exponential increase in cultural strength, in terms of the culture's influence over people, and its staying power. All of this occurs from potentiation, which is the core to both the cancer dynamic and the culture dynamic. Whenever you see a rapidly developing and dramatic event, the first thing you look for to understand what's going on is potentiation. Every time you get on a plane, you experience the effect of potentiation, in terms of what enables planes to fly. Potentiation is essential to how jet engines operate or how a supercharger or turbocharger on a car functions. On a jet engine, air enters the front of the engine where blades that are attached to a shaft compress the air and push it into the combustion chamber. The burning gases expand and rush through a set of blades or turbines at the back of the engine. These blades are attached to the same shaft that the intake blades are attached to, creating a feedback loop where the rear blades spin up the intake blades and increase the pressure in the combustion chamber, which, when ignited, pushes gases even faster through the rear turbine blades. This cycle then repeats itself, increasing the thrust out of the back of the engine. This loop or feedback effect is potentiation, which dramatically increases the thrust out of the engine to propel the aircraft forward. As such, potentiation is based upon feedback loops to create a dynamic.

A sales example is seen when a seller organizes several meetings with several client individuals at about the same time. Perhaps the seller is meeting with one or two people, an executive sponsor is meeting with a client individual, and perhaps a technical support specialist is meeting with a client person—all within a couple of days. While the meetings have different specific topics, they all work to a common sales theme that reflects client-centric value. When all the discussions have taken place, it's not uncommon for client individuals to speak to one another about the supplier. This creates buzz due to the feedback loops of these post-meeting discussions where individuals are talking to individuals absent the seller. The sales technique is called milestone stacking where the overall sales impact is much greater than the sum of the parts or the sum of the sales impact for each meeting. The result is significantly increased sales momentum and pipeline velocity. It is producing competitive advantage not from what is being sold, but how it's being sold, in terms of milestone stacking tactics.

Milestone stacking is not something that we developed, but rather borrowed from the world of Special Operations (SpecOps). SpecOps refers to missions conducted by a relatively small number of highly skilled warfighters that think, plan, and operate in unconventional ways. Given that their run time is usually short and that they can end up taking on a much larger and better equipped adversary force, these teams depend on an asymmetric advantage, or force multiplier, to succeed. Where they find this advantage is with the potentiation generated by the interrelationships and interdependencies of simplicity, speed, security, repetition, surprise, and purpose. These factors, identified by William H. McRaven in his book, *Spec Ops: Case Studies in Special Operations Warfare: Theory and Practice*, coupled with new innovation, violence of action, and other methods enable a Special Forces team to achieve relative superiority very quickly in a fight where a distinctive advantage over the enemy is achieved.

One of these methods is milestone stacking where a number of mission milestones are tactically achieved simultaneously. The tactical effect of this stacking is to disproportionately advance to relative superiority much faster than if the milestones were accomplished in serial fashion. Just as in the earlier sales example, tactical feedback loops are established to amplify the result, which will work in any competitive environment where potentiation, driven by the confluence of events or factors, creates a "perfect storm."

Perhaps one of the most dramatic examples of potentiation is the sinking of the *Titanic* where the coming together or confluence of specific elements combined to potentiate each other and doom the boat. No one element was really significant, but combined, they tell a different story. First of all, the *Titanic* was traveling too fast, as the captain wanted to break the speed record to New York. This reduced reaction time when an iceberg was spotted. Second, multiple warnings of icebergs were ignored, as the boat was considered unsinkable. Next, the lookout on watch had no binoculars and it was a very dark night, which together shortened reaction time to any drifting ice that could be a threat. In addition, the sea was very calm. This meant that no water was splashing up against the icebergs that would have created a white foam visible at quite a distance. This also reduced reaction time.

When the lookout in the crow's nest finally spotted the iceberg dead ahead, he rang the lookout bell and informed the bridge. The quarter-master was then ordered to turn the boat to port. This was accomplished by stopping the center engine and propeller that was directly in front of the rudder. At close to the same time, the port engine was apparently reversed, creating a push-pull configuration of the outward propellers to rotate the boat. The problem was that all this created turbulent water around the rudder, reducing its effectiveness and compromising the turning ability of the boat. With a disproportionately short reaction time, stopping or turning was not possible. Contact with the iceberg came quickly, as an ice spur under the water line ripped into the starboard side of the hull.

As you can see, it was a combination of factors or elements that together produced a result that was highly disproportionate to the elements themselves. But the potentiation didn't stop there. The loss of life was exponentially increased by potentiation, as well. The rivets that secured the plates of steal that made up the hull were one level of quality below what should have been used, causing them to break loose too easily. And, there were too few of them. In addition, the metallurgy of the steal hull plates made them too brittle in cold water. These factors contributed to the breaking open of hull pieces without first bending and the tearing of seams that connected plates, opening them up to leakage that greatly exceeded what the pumps could handle. On top of that, the evacuation was poorly managed, there weren't enough life boats, and leadership in the crisis was essentially nonexistent. All these factors, and others, drove the crisis dynamic through potentiation and contributed to the heavy loss of life.

The Potentiating Factors of a Looking Glass Culture

A Looking Glass Culture has a personality that tends to dehumanize customers, discounting and subordinating them to itself. We read a lot today about technology dehumanizing people, but this is only one piece of the puzzle. In addition to people and time potentiating each other within a culture, there are four other factors that fuel the culture dynamic through potentiation:

- **Intimacy without Engagement** – Social networking has created a phenomenon where the human need for herding or fellowship with others can be satisfied without physical contact. Sharing thoughts, ideas, feelings, and events with unlimited numbers of others in the blink of an eye has now been technologically enabled. And responses are equally as quick, responses that rate the merit of anything shared with a possible thumbs up or "like" that speaks to how popular a person is; producing a feeling of self-worth. And, the faster the positive responses, the more they're worth, driving an increased short-term mindset. As time and sincerity diminish, this works against building real client relationships.

- **Driven to Distraction** – The 24/7 hyperconnectivity with sellers receiving, for example, two hundred to four hundred emails per day consumes time and sales capacity, while perpetuating itself with emails and generic-value positioning documents sent to clients to save time by avoiding actually calling on customers. Again, technologically enabled, these selling gestures create the illusion of client contact but confusing activity, speed, and scale with progress. And again, a short-term mindset.

- **Cultural Preoccupation** – Compliance with cultural norms at deep emotional levels drives an inward focus at the expense of clients and sales effectiveness. The irrational becomes rational as self-deception protects cultural inhabitants from the anxiety of not adhering to what is expected company behavior.

- **Self-entitlement** – The survival response of putting yourself first, protecting your career, internal relationships, and reputation for being a team player projects onto the organization, intensifying the inward focus of the company. And as the pressure of the environment increases due to decreasing sales effectiveness, the self-protect instinct grows stronger and spreads to other cultural inhabitants.

The effect of these four factors is not equal to their sum but is exponentially greater as they reinforce each other to produce disproportionate culture growth, strength, and the ability to resist change. They not only dehumanize clients, but when that happens over a long enough period of time, it is our view that the culture also begins to dehumanize sellers and sales managers—showing little care for their opinions, experience, ability, or career wellbeing. This is the destructive power and dynamic of a Looking Glass Culture.

While the Looking Glass Culture and *Titanic* examples of potentiating destructive power are inherently tragic in today's world, the Zuza story is not. Fighting fire with fire, a protocol was developed that created a therapeutic dynamic to fight the cancer dynamic. It consisted of three core elements: Dexamethasone, that was administered according to a math model supporting minimum dosing to therapeutic effect; Thalidomide, which was actually banned for veterinary use; and the Reishi mushroom. By the grace of God, the protocol worked, stopping proliferation, and neutralizing the cancer's ability to defeat apoptosis for a long enough time for all cancer cells to die. The remission was very durable with no sign of the cancer after extensive and repeated testing. The Zuza protocol then became the basis for a human trial, approved by the Institutional Review Board (IRB),[1] for fifty multiple myeloma patients over a two-year period. The FDA also approved an IND (Investigational New Drug) single patient clinical trial for Zuza using Revlimid (Lenalidomide), which was a new drug at the time. Today, this approach has become the standard of care for people and

---

1   Under FDA regulations, an IRB is a group that has been formally designated to review and monitor biomedical research involving human subjects.

while the immunomodulation approach was based upon science, it was driven by a caring attitude and commitment. It's also caring that drives CX (as we discussed in Chapter 6) and sales results, as it's a powerful source of competitive advantage that is nontraditional in Looking Glass Cultures.

The Pace of Culture Change

The Culture Change Process. *When driving behavioral change in people, there is an optimal pace to effect change that is sustainable, just as is the case in nature and society.* The same holds true with culture. The personification of culture provides you with added insight as to who it is and how it operates because it's made up of people. In all these cases, culture, society, and nature, equilibrium needs to be maintained so that the environment will remain stable. But at the same time, change disturbs equilibrium, which results in forces immediately working to restore it. These forces exist as feedback to the change and can achieve stabilization by stopping the change initiative or by institutionalizing the change so that it becomes part of the culture with equilibrium once again restored. Therefore, the key to effective and sustainable culture change is to drive small, highly focused changes within the Looking Glass Culture that are directly linked to improving sales effectiveness relative to specific sales opportunities.

At that point a specific change needs to be socialized within the sales organization and with the appropriate Foxes for broader adoption, which is the institutionalizing piece of the process. With equilibrium restored, the stage is set for the next sustainable culture change initiative to produce a smooth progression of change: a modulated continuum of culture changes driven by successful sales initiatives where the frequency of these initiatives is determined by what the culture can absorb. Basically, any culture-change effort should not precede full stabilization of the previous change.

The Background to This Process. *In society, nature, and culture, the resistance to change will directly relate to the magnitude of the change and the speed with which it's being driven.* In 2013, the Egyptian military removed President Mohamed Morsi, who was rapidly driving significant change with a new constitution based upon Islamic Law and a consolidation of power that was too much too fast. *The New York Times* wrote, "For Mr. Morsi, it was a bitter and ignominious end to a tumultuous year of bruising political battles that ultimately alienated millions of Egyptians. Having won a narrow victory, his critics say, he broke his promises of an inclusive government and repeatedly demonized his opposition as traitors. With the economy crumbling, and with shortages of electricity and fuel, anger at the government mounted."[2] In addition, Morsi made the mistake of not first building support with all the appropriate Foxes, particularly in the military. Also noteworthy is the feedback loop that consisted of the Egyptian people who elected Morsi then driving the Egyptian military, en masse, to intervene and depose him—thus correcting the problem and restoring equilibrium.

In nature, you see the principles at work with equilibrium expressed as homeostasis. According to the *Encyclopedia Britannica*, homeostasis is "any self-regulating process by which biological systems tend

---

2 www.nytimes.com/2013/07/04/world/middleeast/egypt.html

to maintain stability while adjusting to conditions that are optimal for survival. If homeostasis is successful, life continues; if unsuccessful, disaster or death ensues. The stability attained is actually a dynamic equilibrium, in which continuous change occurs yet relatively uniform conditions prevail." It goes on to provide the following example: "Body temperature control in humans is one of the most familiar examples of homeostasis. Normal body temperature hovers around 37 °C (98.6 °F), but a number of factors can affect this value, including exposure to the elements, hormones, metabolic rate, and disease, leading to excessively high or low body temperatures. The hypothalamus in the brain regulates body temperature, and feedback about body temperature from the body is carried through the bloodstream to the brain, which results in adjustments in breathing rate, blood sugar levels, and metabolic rate. In contrast, reduced activity, perspiration, and heat-exchange processes that permit more blood to circulate near the skin surface contribute to heat loss. Heat loss is reduced by insulation, decreased circulation to the skin, clothing, shelter, and external heat sources."[3]

To look at the pace of change from a team perspective, I'd like to take you back to Mt. Kilimanjaro. My team's approach to the summit was to traverse the mountain over a period of seven days, which would help us acclimate to the altitude. It began with a steep hike up the rain forest to the Shira Plateau at 10,000 feet, then across the mountain and up to high camp at Barafu, 15,500 feet. At midnight we made the summit attempt to Uhuru Peak at 19,341 feet, which took eleven hours. On the way, back at the Shira Plateau, we found ourselves climbing

---

3 www.britannica.com/science/homeostasis

in parallel with a German team. We had set up the tents and were preparing for very bad weather that we expected that night when we observed the German team climbing some of the steep verticals in the area. It was impressive, and while we were keeping very busy to both get ready for nightfall and accelerate acclimation to the altitude, we wondered if we should be climbing as well. But something told us not to overdrive so early in the climb.

For days this level of activity was the routine of the Germans who were very disciplined, well prepared with good equipment, and in great shape, being strong and athletic. We all thought that these guys would fly to the summit, but fast forward to the approach on Barafu and the German team went missing. It turned out that they had been suffering from headaches, vomiting, dizziness, and extreme fatigue. Moving too hard and too fast with low oxygen levels had brought on altitude sickness, the number one cause of death on Mt. Kilimanjaro. It's a problem where there is only one cure: to get off the mountain. For the German team, it was a pace issue that led to defeat. In sales, it would be like trying to force-close a customer who's not ready to make a buy decision—or trying to drive too much culture change too quickly. There is no substitute for finding the right pace.

At Barafu, the two of us and a guide knew that pacing the summit attempt would be an issue, as our food that night turned out to be contaminated and we had no sleep. It was so cold that I was wearing everything I had and every time I would begin to fall asleep, my blood pressure would drop, and a severe headache would wake me. This was not just an inconvenience; hypothermia is the second most frequent cause of death on Mt. Kilimanjaro. That said, at midnight we were able to set off for the summit. The key was to reach 17,000 feet at about sunup. Get there sooner and our pace would be too fast, meaning that we could run out of energy and strength before reaching the summit. Get there later, and the sun might raise the freeze point, creating rock fall and avalanche risk, which is the third cause of death on the mountain.

Thankfully, we made it to the top of the crater wall with only a quarter of a mile to hike 250 vertical feet. Problem was that at that altitude, around 19,000 feet, we could only go six steps at a time with three full breaths per step. Then, we had to stop and rest. It took two hours to make it to Uhuru Peak where we signed the summit book and looked out in one direction to see the Maasai Mara in Kenya, and in the opposite direction to see Tanzania. It was beautiful. We then headed down five miles to a base camp, got our certificates, and looked back on one exciting adventure.

Managing the Pace of Change in Moving a Looking Glass Culture to a Client-Centric Culture. *One of the hallmarks of a Looking Glass Culture is the inward company focus that it drives at the direct expense of customer interest, focus, understanding, priority, and face-to-face interaction.* Consistent with this is the generic one-to-many market messaging that is often supplier-focused in terms of its capabilities and accomplishments. In this context, a specific culture change initiative might be to identify a specific group of clients that fit a specific criteria, for example, accounts that generate 10 million euro or more for your company per year. Or, it might consist of a group of clients that purchases solutions from a particular product/service line.

By focusing on a narrow but important band of customers, you reduce the magnitude of the change and, therefore, reduce the resistance to change. Next, you propose that all sales proposals and presentations be reviewed by sales management to ensure that they are client-centric. That is, focus on client value first and how it will be achieved and not on the ten reasons clients should buy from you. It's establishing an understanding of the customers' business and what's important to them, in terms of the business value that you will provide.

With positive client feedback and sales success, you move to formalize culture change with organizational support secured by specific Foxes in the company. For example, you might work to secure their support to include the proposal and presentation client-centric review in every pipeline and sales forecasting discussion for the specific group of clients. This is the institutionalizing piece of the process. When this new practice is established, equilibrium will be restored, and sustainability assured.

Summary of Chapter 8

In this chapter, you've been introduced to the concept of personifying culture to better understand how it actually works, what drives it, what threatens it, and how it protects itself. You've seen its strength and endurance, along with how it is both intelligent and emotional where feelings can be more important than facts, and how it demonstrates a defensive mindset, ready to destroy or purge anything that attempts to drive unwanted change. This makes changing a Looking Glass Culture a formidable task, as potentiation provides it with significant power. Whenever dramatic and sudden events occur, often unexpectedly, potentiation can be at work, as specific factors come together to quickly produce a disproportionate result.

In a Looking Glass Culture, these factors and their support by powerful people can actually cause the dehumanizing of customers over time, and as sales effectiveness declines, the dehumanizing and indictment of sellers and sales managers occurs as well. This brings into focus the need to carefully pace culture change, as in any change initiative, resistance is proportional to the magnitude and speed of change.

This sets the stage to next look at pursuit team configuration and operations to advance important deal sales campaigns and the development of major accounts in balance with creating a Client-Centric Culture. This balance is based upon the principle of winning the battle and growing in strength. That is, winning an important deal and, in the process, building the right culture will help win future deals.

PART THREE

Winning Important Deals

9

The Pursuit Team

"If everyone is moving forward together, then success takes care of itself."—Henry Ford

In today's company cultures, the success of a large deal pursuit campaign is not determined by strategy and flawless execution of its tactics alone, but by the configuration, quality, and effectiveness of the pursuit team. This is not to discount the importance of strategy and tactics, but to instead recognize that the trajectory of a large deal compete curve will be set before the campaign is ever launched. Team configuration and quality is simply having the right personalities with the right capabilities on the team. Personality configuration is actually at the top of the list, before capabilities. People need to get along, work together, and collaborate, which is consistent with gig culture that also takes it to the extreme.

It's not just having the right personal attributes, but also the right individual philosophies and work styles that can actually be inconsistent with gig culture but conducive to effective teamwork, particularly in a distributed work environment. Attributes that play into this include flexibility in attitude and thinking; conflict resolution through a willingness to listen, understand, and relate to different points of view; drive and determination; a positive and constructive mindset; and so on.

Capabilities can be considered as both general and specific. General capabilities include leadership and strategic-thinking ability, communication skills, an analytical attention to detail, knowing the company culture, political savvy, and more. Specific capabilities often include knowledge of specific industries and clients, products and offerings, technologies, business functions like finance or manufacturing, writing and presenting skills, and so forth. But all of this does not necessarily make for an effective team, in terms of producing sales results in a timely manner. Also required is the right team focus, ability to communicate with people outside the team, particularly company executives, effective operational security protocols, and most importantly, team unity, in terms of philosophy and collective mindset.

Now, if there were no internal resistance within the company, this would be enough. But there will be resistance as important sales campaigns in today's companies will likely have to take on company culture in some way or fashion. This is something that you can count on. Any important deal pursuit team is going to run into some level of inward company focus that is insensitive to client needs and resistant to change, as internal politics and human behavior express themselves and tend to bog down and complicate efforts to win very important and competitive opportunities. A pursuit team must have the collective willingness and ability to operate in a countercultural manner, which brings us back to team configuration and involving the right people who can effectively punch through cultural obstacles. When this happens, the pursuit team will be engaging in a Monkey Dance.

The Monkey Dance

Remember our primate behavior example where the monkeys in a cage had been behaviorally conditioned? Well, hang on then. When a pursuit team runs into a disagreement with a company individual who is inflicted with cultural preoccupation, they will likely be pushing on some aspect of a Looking Glass Culture. It may be an executive who insists the team take an approach that is counter to the pursuit effort or to what the client requires or one that is contraindicated to whatever the pursuit team lead feels is required to win the business.

This is a strategic problem that has the potential to derail the entire pursuit. It's a situation that occurs, to varying degrees, far more often than you would likely think. And when it happens, the executive is often adamant about it, as he is in a mode of self-deception. Again, this fear-based denial reduces the anxiety of not complying with company culture and what is expected, often induced by career concerns; not putting the company first or not aligning with the views of a very senior and powerful executive. This is anxiety anesthetized by rationalizing away your team's argument and logic. When this is the case and civil discourse fails, you're in a Monkey Dance. Commonsense will not prevail, no common understanding will be achieved, and there may be no respect for the client's views or your arguments.

What you could see is excessive persuasion, expressed as a directive if the individual has authority over you. This can happen in private or (if the executive is insecure and short on leadership ability or doesn't have authority over you) in front of the pursuit team. Certainly, the hope is that this will not occur, but in today's gig culture, it's best to be prepared, as you can easily find yourself in a lose-lose situation.

If you accept the directive of the executive it could compromise the pursuit campaign and lose the deal. On the other hand, not accepting the directive could possibly put your career at risk. *This is a Monkey Dance. It is a form of confrontation and disagreement that is not driven by logic or rational thought on one or both sides.* It's based upon primate instinct and emotions. Logic will often not prevail over arrogance and fear in situations where you don't have authority. This lose-lose situation will have you in a box. And while it appears on the surface to be irresolvable with no way out, there is a way to manage it.

The first step to managing this problem is to get out of the box. *The way to be successful in a Monkey Dance is to not be part of it.* Listen, be respectful, and advise the executive that you will carefully consider his views. Then, get to a supporter or ally in the corporate Power Base and brief that person on the situation. Ask her to quickly speak with the executive and get him to quietly back down. This puts power against power—not your power, but that of a supporter who has significant influence, a person who is an extended part of your pursuit team because you set it up that way when you configured your pursuit team. As such, you're not jumping over the executive's head, but simply working with a key team member for her opinion and guidance. She is an advisor to your team—or what is often called an executive sponsor—who can get you out of the line of fire by getting you out of the Monkey Dance. For her, this becomes a discussion between executives.

It might get emotionally charged, but it won't get out of hand. That's because of the balance of power. Monkey Dances are almost always between one with and one without significant power. And when you're the one without power, the prognosis is never good. This is one of the real responsibilities of an executive sponsor, but you'll never see it written anywhere. What you will see are the classic executive sponsor role responsibilities, often sporadically fulfilled, if at all, as they relate to a major account or the pursuit of a large deal.

That said, where you will likely need her help the most is internally to avoid a Monkey Dance and externally to interface with client executives. On the Monkey Dance side of the role, she'll be addressing the executive to contain the situation, which is not something that you'll likely be equipped to handle. For example, the executive might sincerely believe that you are wrong in your approach with the client and that it needs to be corrected. Perhaps he really doesn't understand the situation; doesn't have the ability or experience to understand it or doesn't want to understand it or be educated.

Many times, Monkey Dances are initiated by executives who have no sales experience. It could also be that he is very insecure and needs to exert dominance, particularly if he has given you a directive in public. It might also be that the executive is managing up; supporting what he believes is the view of a powerful senior executive who might be out of touch with what is going on in the field and with the client. With your executive sponsor quietly de-escalating the situation, no one loses face. No one is embarrassed. If the executive gave you the directive in front of your team, simply advise them that the executive's recommendation is being addressed and that the team should proceed as planned. Make no more of it. *The desired outcome of a Monkey Dance is containment, de-escalation, and removal of the obstacle. It is not to win or make public anything.*

The Monkey Dance is another example of adapting a concept from a different domain and applying it to provide further insight and guidance. In the world of adversarial conflict between people, the Monkey Dance is a form of social confrontation that has the potential to escalate into physical violence. Rory Miller, in his book *Facing Violence: Preparing for the Unexpected,* introduces the Monkey Dance to assist readers in avoiding violence by managing down an emotionally charged situation. As you know, emotions often rule when people are under pressure, which is also the case with culture when it's under pressure. Absent the reference to violence, this is particularly true when a pursuit lead is in a lose-lose box fighting a Looking Glass Culture, thus, the applicability of Rory's concept.

Team Configuration

Team Building Step One: Configure the core team, which consists of people essential to the pursuit campaign. Recognizing that knowledge consists of information and skill, what areas of knowledge are required to support team operations? Start with team leadership. Who will serve in the Command & Control (C2) function as team lead for the important deal pursuit? It may be you, if you're the account executive who has been covering the account. But, if you're somewhat new to sales or haven't had much experience on key sales pursuits, we recommend you bring on a deputy team lead that has strong sales experience. This is a person who could also carry another role on the team working side-by-side with you, just as a COO would do with a CEO.

Having an experienced "right hand" is never a bad thing on a large deal that can be highly competitive. Remember that good leadership is based on good delegation, and of all the team functions, C2 is the most important.

Have you ever attended the symphony? Prior to the performance, the orchestra warms up with musicians playing instruments, horns blowing, and scales soaring. It's nothing less than a musical expression of chaos; dissonant and discordant orchestral noise. Then the orchestra leader steps on stage and through his direction musical beauty emerges. This is the C2 role on the pursuit team. It is not just managing every team function, but integrating and coordinating each function to produce a symphony of pursuit perfection.

Team Building Step Two: With leadership support nailed down, it's time to complete the core team. Keep in mind that the core team consists of people who are, again, essential to winning the deal. Be aware that often many individuals will want to jump on board to represent whatever they do in the company or to be associated with an important win. You must filter out these people. When they are needed, you'll bring them in. But they should not be part of the standing core team. We see way too many pursuit teams that consist of fifty to sixty people, which is the first most common leadership mistake. And it's a mistake that leads to the second most common problem: leadership by committee.

I recently met with a senior corporate executive for an international professional services firm who described their sales forecasting process for large deals as one that consisted of frequent conference calls involving thirty to fifty people that often run for about three hours each. The high attendance level and long duration of these calls reflect two dimensions that illustrate the following points:

- **Consensus management** – There's a desire to involve everyone who could possibly have an opinion for maximum information gathering. The problem here is that not all information is valid and not all information is relevant to accuracy and timely sales forecasting. Inclusion management has its place, but the world of sales is not always one of them.

- **Management by committee** – This is for self-validation through the accepted common view. The problem is that the common view is often not the right view.

- **Politics** – As powerful people weigh in with their opinions it can cause others to be naturally reluctant to disagree or correct what is being stated. This creates distortion, confusion, and misdirection that complicates and obfuscates the sales forecasting process.

All of this reflects a Looking Glass Culture, which will work against proper pursuit team configuration that should result in the core team with a nucleus at its center.

The Core Team Nucleus

The pursuit team nucleus is made up of the C2 pursuit lead, the team's executive sponsor, and a third person. We mentioned earlier that large deal pursuits are the canary in the mine, as they relate to making culture visible. Sellers are often the first to know that a Looking Glass Culture has formed by its impact on sales—that is, if they are not themselves preoccupied with bad culture. This also applies to new sales hires who are brought in to "fix" the decline-in-sales problem or replace performing sellers who have left the company. If their experiential frame of reference does not include selling in a good Client-Centric Culture, they will quickly become part of the problem. This brings us to the third role in the pursuit team nucleus.

If sellers having one foot in the company and one in the client organization is good, having half a foot in the company and one and a half in the client environment is better. This is where the industry advisor comes in relative to the client's business. Often this person is viewed as an employee but can actually be a contractor (perhaps because the supplier doesn't have a critical mass of industry market share to support a full-time person). In any event, it suggests that he has not been living in a bad culture and has been exposed to many clients in the particular industry of focus. With more of an outside-in perspective on the supplier company and his knowledge of the client industry and major players, he often knows what he's dealing with and what works with clients and what is irrational. Spotting a supplier Looking Glass Culture is fairly quick. And as such, he knows the power of setting up the pursuit team properly, including the right executive sponsor for the team.

In addition, the industry advisor may have worked with the procurement advisor if one has been hired by the client to manage the procurement process. The mismatch in culture between supplier and customer has become such a global problem that third-party companies are now often required to represent clients on large purchases, managing the entire procurement process. This has given birth to a new industry. It also makes the industry advisor more than an industry advisor. He not only knows the industry, its leaders, what drives them, emerging trends, and more, but is likely to know a great deal more about the client than anyone on the pursuit team, particularly if they are living in a Looking Glass Culture. Industry advisors talk to everyone in the business. They work in the white space, moving around the industry within companies, clients, and procurement advisor organizations with some degree of freedom. They are relationship builders who often carry a lot of influence with pursuit teams, clients, and procurement advisors. In some cases, the industry advisor informally serves as the deputy team lead, as that right-hand person to the pursuit lead.

The pursuit team nucleus is now in place with the pursuit lead, executive sponsor, and industry advisor. In the next chapter you'll be hearing more about industry advisors directly from the source. Rj Smith, advisor for the gaming and hospitality industry, will be contributing to Chapter 11 with his observations on culture alignment and change, the role of the industry advisor, the value provided, and the challenges to producing that value. It will be a rare look into the opportunities and frustrations of supplier-client cultural misalignment, including the procurement advisor who is essentially an extension of the client.

The Core Team

Solution and Technology Specialists

With the core nucleus configured, other key roles can be added. Solution and technology specialists will play an important role in fully understanding client requirements, advising the client, and configuring competitively differentiated solutions, often working closely with the industry advisor and other team members. This is not a one-shot function. Large and important deals are highly competitive and dynamic in their nature, which makes this role an ongoing one throughout the campaign cycle.

Financial Specialist

The finance person can help manage the business development expense and assist in quantifying value to the client. This may involve estimating potential increases in client revenue, acceleration of revenue, increases in margin based upon a possible reduction in client working capital or cost reduction, impact on earnings per share, and other quantitative expressions of value, including risk reduction. The financial role is also key to reviewing client financials, building financial models relative to solutions provided, and qualifying the opportunity to justify the business development expense. Financial models that relate to a solution are particularly important, as they may include creative approaches to helping the client manage their budget requirements, particularly when preparing for the BAFO (Best And Final Offer) stage late in the buying process. It's at this time that the pursuit campaign will be peaking with a client decision about to be made—a time when mistakes cannot be made.

Research Analyst

The analyst also plays an important deep-dive role. You'll need to understand the client; their business, direction, priorities, and culture, the latter dictating not *what* needs to be accomplished for the customer, but *how* it needs to be accomplished. The analyst will also work with the industry advisor to understand the client's industry, who they compete with, the industry leaders, emerging industry trends, and so on.

If you're the seller on the account, you may have a lot of this information. Or, your industry advisor may have what you need. Still, there will be an ongoing need for research, not only on the client and their industry, but also on the competition. And this is not a one-shot deal. The research effort is ongoing throughout the sales campaign. Deep dives will be required into areas like the client's political landscape, which can be very dynamic with changes in the situational Power Base. Constant monitoring of industry analyst reports and client executive presentations, articles, and interviews may also require deep dives of research to develop insights that could be key to campaign success. Therefore, you will want to be certain that you have sufficient analyzing capacity between yourself, your industry advisor, and your analyst. It's also useful to note that the analyst and financial roles can sometimes be combined if, for example, the analyst has a financial background.

Bid Manager

The bid manager will look after RFP (Request for Proposal) compliance and all administrative aspects of the pursuit, bringing in auxiliary resources such as technical writers and creative types to produce proposals and structure presentations, along with other tasks that take place at the direction of the pursuit lead. From a team perspective, the bid manager is the gateway to accessing all necessary auxiliary resources that don't belong on the core team, but are necessary from time to time, again, under the direction of the team lead. That said, it's also the responsibility of the bid manager to ensure that all auxiliary support people focus on the team mission and not prioritize what they do or their business objective above the pursuit team mission. This ensures that all contributions are highly relevant and keeps the core team as lean and focused as possible, while protecting core team manageability and capacity.

Legal and Commercial Management

Bringing on a legal person with knowledge of the law and risk management, along with a commercial individual who can understand and manage the business impact of various legal provisions, is also key. Often, the view is to bring these people in late in the sales cycle, post down select, but we advise that they be made a part of the core team and be involved from the beginning—not necessarily in all of the meetings, but in many with the client and the client procurement advisor, if one is present. This enables them to develop an in-depth understanding of all aspects of the campaign, client, and procurement advisor, as well as have the opportunity to build relationships with the appropriate people.

By proactively identifying key issues to be addressed in the final negotiations of the deal, the pursuit lead is then able to tie the desired approach to addressing these issues to any concessions made before legal and business negotiations formally begin. This simplifies the negotiations. Keep in mind that on sophisticated deals there are many legal documents that go well beyond a Master Services Agreement (MSA) that all need to work together, comprising the right legal architecture.

Now, it's time to select and brief your executive sponsor. When pursuing an important deal, this person should be in the corporate executive Power Base. Go Fox hunting and find that individual, being very careful not to engage with a Jackal. Talk about the possible need to engage in a Monkey Dance, explain it, along with any concerns you might have if you're living in a Looking Glass Culture. Pursuing large, very important opportunities is going to be highly visible and highly political within your company. Be proactive and Fox-like yourself. Win the battle before it's fought and avoid a Monkey Dance.

Summary of Chapter 9

In this chapter, you've been introduced to one of the most challenging situations a seller can face—the Monkey Dance. When a Looking Glass Culture asserts itself in the pursuit of an important deal, it puts the pursuit team lead in a lose-lose position. Either he sells in a manner consistent with culture and management directive, putting the deal at risk, or challenges the culture and directive, putting his job security at risk. The solution for this lies with the pursuit team configuration and roles that are established in advance.

As a pursuit team lead, getting out of this box and avoiding a Monkey Dance is achieved through the direct support of an executive sponsor or other powerful executive who can intercede with the manager giving the inappropriate directive. Such a directive may be to attempt to close the business this quarter when the pursuit lead knows it's not possible from the client's point of view. Or it may be to alter the proposed solution in a manner that is inconsistent with RFP requirements. The result of having the executive sponsor work the issue is containment, de-escalation, and removal of the campaign obstacle. With this role in mind, you now have a recommended core team structure to drive campaign success and keep you out of debilitating Monkey Dances.

In the next chapter, you'll see how to characterize and define the team mission statement, which identifies the value of the pursuit and provides guidance in an ability to always know what sales activities are directionally correct to winning.

10

Pursuit Team Mission

"To succeed in your mission, you must have single-minded devotion to your goal."—A. P. J. Abdul Kalam

The cornerstone to pursuit team focus and achievement is the mission statement. It consists of three main components and a number of subcomponents that every member of the core pursuit team will need to understand and personally internalize. Recognize that it's not a static document, but a living, changing, and dynamic expression of team purpose. This is the responsibility of the pursuit team lead, focusing on:

1. **Sales Objective**
   a. *What will be sold* – What are you selling and why?
   b. *When it will be sold* – This is the most critical component to the Sales Objective. Too many sellers superficially ask the question and leave it there. If the client explains that a decision will be made at a certain time, you must do a deep dive. Ask who within the account determines timing and what the implications would be if the decision were not made at that time. Inquire as to which client individuals and client departments

would be most affected if the decision slipped. And then, stay close to events to determine the likelihood of slippage. Your resource planning to support the pursuit campaign and delivery of the solution can be significantly affected by close timing, as well as increasing your business development costs and the risk of losing to a no-decision or the competition.

c. *For what price* – Also note any performance-based revenue potential.

2. **Extended Significance of this Deal to the Company**
   a. *How this deal will produce future business* – This, along with price, creates key context to accurately justify business development expenses, allocation of resources, and future concessions and discounts. A large deal can often be pivotal in leading to the penetration of new markets, creating new revenue streams, accelerating revenue, and establishing a critical mass of market share that produces a barrier to entry for competitors in specific market sectors.
   b. *What winning this deal means to each pursuit team member* – This speaks to each core team member's personal and professional aspirations. How will pursuit success impact each person both in the short term and long term? Commissions, bonuses, promotions, career advancement potential, balanced lifestyle, desired relocation, assignment of key projects and responsibilities, or increasing budgets are all possible examples.

3. **Point at which Relative Superiority will be Achieved**
   a. *Who the likely primary competitor is* – This is an assessment

made both before and after down select, as to which competitor is your most significant threat. With this, you're able to repeatedly run a differentiation analysis against that company that compares your strengths and weakness to its, which becomes the basis for your compete strategy.

b. ***At what point in time will a distinctive advantage be achieved over the competition*** – This is the point in the pursuit campaign where your compete strategy enables you to see the defeat of your primary competitor. It's not done at that juncture, but how events will unfold to bring you to victory will be visible. It is a point in time when you can see the next several moves to checkmate. But, instead of referring to it as "check," as we would in chess, we consider it the prime objective to any important sales campaign. It's a post down select achievement that signals victory that when realized early in the campaign dramatically reduces competitive vulnerability.

c. ***How will this be accomplished*** – This is the companion to the "when," looking at the "how" relative superiority will be achieved. For example, it might be the establishment of an informal agreement in principle with a client Fox that takes place before any structured procurement policies and procedures have been put in place, e.g., an agreement in principle that is based upon your bringing new and unexpected business value to the client based upon new innovation. All this occurs proactively with the understanding that there will be no prohibition on submitting an alternate bid that perhaps changes the ground rules, as an indirect compete strategy.

159

Team Culture

Supporting the team mission is a culture within a culture. If your team is living in a Client-Centric Culture, all is good, and the task is to conceptually leverage or focus the strengths of the company culture onto the pursuit effort with customer obsession. But if your team is living in a Looking Glass or Confused Culture, you can plan on one or more Monkey Dances, as a boundary condition is going to exist between the pursuit team and the company environment. This doesn't mean that you compromise your team culture or efforts to improve compatibility with company culture. Instead, it means being very clear about your team culture and how you will operate, while being prepared for the Monkey Dance. To create this clarity, we'll define team culture in terms of four factors: beliefs, values, morals, and ethics. These team factors need to be made relevant to the pursuit effort and each team member should embrace and reflect them in all actions and behaviors:

Beliefs – Something that you confidently trust to be true

Values – Something's level of importance to you

Morals – Behavior that you hold to be right or wrong

Ethics – Behavior that is generally viewed as acceptable based upon universal fairness

So how does all this work? Like the core team concept of involving only individuals essential to an important deal pursuit, the following is the core to the pursuit team culture involving only those factors and principles critical to the successful formation and operation of the pursuit team. First, we look at principles that the team must trust to be true, hold to be very important, and know to be fair (Beliefs + Values + Ethics):

Serving

- The pursuit team exists to serve the client and your company where serve means contribute to the client and your company in a manner worthy of trust. *It is not dictating to the client, nor is it accepting whatever the client wants from you.*
- Serving the client should be done in balance with serving your company. Value to the client should be balanced over an appropriate timeframe with value to your company. Investing in and solving a client problem that is of commercial value to them, but not charging them for it or gaining some kind of value for your company violates fairness.
- The physical process of serving is to determine how to make a contribution to the client's business in a specific area, assess its value not from your point of view, but from the client's perspective, and then confirm that the service provided is in balance with the business interests of your company, in order to maintain fairness.

Sounds simple, but to accomplish this on a consistent basis requires leadership, strength, and confidence. Specifically, to tie all team factors together you must

- Know your client as well as you know your company. Since you don't live in the client organization, this means you are committed to ongoing deep research into the client's business and industry. You must be relentless or obsessed with under-standing everything possible about their company, culture, and people.

- Be ready, willing, and able to respectfully and diplomatically disagree with the client when you know by experience that what they are proposing is wrong, even though it is not what they want to hear. And be able to back up your position with credible facts.

- Never communicate false information, omit information, or exaggerate anything that might mislead the client to any degree, directly or indirectly. Everything you say or communicate must be complete and true.

- Never rationalize authority over the client. For example, if you're an industry leader, that doesn't give you the right to be insensitive to client requirements when they don't align with your product and service strengths. Resist the view that the client should adapt its business to your solutions, believing that your way is the only right way. There is no place for arrogance in serving.

- Never rationalize professional desire over the client. That is attitudinally subordinating the client's priorities to your prior-ities where, for example, you work to force the client to make a buy decision before they are ready using pressure, fear, or false information. Perhaps it's to close business before the end of the quarter because your management wants it or because you're looking forward to the commission check. But, don't confuse this with encouraging the client to make an early deci-sion through incentives that the client will value.

- Practice transparency whenever appropriate and reasonable, subject to confidentiality requirements, need to know, and professionalism.
- Always protect the integrity of your company's business. Be respectful and professional, but do not let a client "run your business," create inappropriate business risk, or compromise the financial condition of your company.
- *Never allow any of your company executives, managers, or support people to go into the account and not comply with the above.*
- *Never allow a company executive, manager, or support person to enter or interface with the account to address anything dispositive without the knowledge of the team lead.*

There is a lot more that could be said about team culture, particularly given situationally specific considerations. For this reason, it is recommended that the team lead facilitate a team session on the dos and don'ts of team operations, hitting the points mentioned and others judged to be important. This should include non-client facing considerations as well such as Operational Security (OPSEC)—treating pursuit campaign information as confidential—and communication protocols, particularly with company senior management, which is generally the domain of the team lead, along with intra-team communications and collaboration.

Team Integration and Coordination

Few pursuit team leads think about how to formally structure the integration and coordination of the various team functions, but rather simply have everyone present in all internal meetings and as many client-facing activities as possible. The hope is that all this overlap will drive informal collaboration and support the team lead's ability to drive multifunctional discussions whenever necessary. But the goal of team integration goes beyond that and centers on driving pursuit effectiveness and fast response times through increased situational awareness and team agility.

An example of this, again in a different domain, is the F-22 Raptor. This fifth-generation advanced tactical fighter defines air dominance with its combination of speed, stealth, maneuverability, situational awareness, and weapons capability. Unlike other extremely capable fighters, like the F-15 Eagle, the Raptor has the most advanced integrated avionics in the world. Radar, communications, navigation, weapons management, and electronic warfare capabilities are all fully integrated into one coherent Head-Up Display (HUD). Whereas in the Eagle the pilot would have to go through five or six different operations with individual systems to identify, target, and destroy an enemy aircraft, the Raptor does it all in essentially one step. With a high degree of situational awareness coupled with ultra-fast and effective response times, the Raptor actually achieves relative superiority before a battle begins.

Not unlike the Raptor, a pursuit team fighting for an important deal also needs to be ahead of the curve. This means being ahead of the client, anticipating events and leading the procurement process whenever possible, and certainly staying ahead of the competition. This happens through the tight and close integration of team functions that communicate essential and relevant information to one point in a timely and clear manner. In this sense, the words "essential" and "relevant" speak to specific information that is tied to advancing the pursuit team mission. And like a HUD, that information and insight is streamed in near real time to the pursuit team lead with daily succinct updates compiled into one coherent report by the bid manager.

This multi-discipline, connect-the-dots approach seeks to not only pull everything together in a way that quickly and accurately conveys relevant insights, but also promotes intra-team synergies where the potentiation of different functional inputs create an exponential increase in insightfulness earlier in time, well ahead of the competition. For example, your research analyst may have come upon information that suggests that a due diligence exercise may be taking place, which could signal a possible future merger or acquisition with another company. If that's the case, you might infer that the growth strategy that we presented earlier in this book regarding the combination of an inorganic growth driver, such as an acquisition or merger or a sale of assets and an emphasis on scalability, along with digital transformation and cost reduction, could be at play. As a result, a discussion with the research analyst and the team's executive sponsor, facilitated by the team lead, could point to setting up an exploratory meeting with a client executive to test the hypothesis and develop further insight. This could then suggest that an IT outsourcing opportunity might be forthcoming, which causes the team lead to bring in the industry advisor to help fill in any missing pieces.

It could also indicate that the approach to reducing costs through outsourcing will need to be one that supports the inorganic driver in some way, which makes agility in your solution an important factor from the standpoint of speed and flexibility. It also suggests that the size of the deal could grow if the outsourcing were to include the company that the client merges with or acquires. All of this could lead to additional targeted client discussion to develop the thinking. And that might lead to a possible transformation initiative to boost revenue growth, which further directs your client research and discussions, enabling you to demonstrate thought leadership and perhaps actually create an expanded sales opportunity.

And this is happening long before any RFP is issued, giving you the ability to build client relationships, map out the client political landscape, and position business value before the client creates a structured buying environment with a procurement advisor, as an example. But this will likely not happen if a Looking Glass Culture exists and you're forced into a Monkey Dance, which again underscores the importance of setting up and configuring the pursuit team properly.

Summary of Chapter 10

Having discussed pursuit team configuration in chapter 9, this last chapter presented the cornerstone to team success. Often overlooked, even in the largest and most important deal pursuits, is the team's mission statement. This is a living, breathing document that provides purpose, meaning, and direction to everything the team will do to win business.

By "**purpose**," we mean the intent and resolve of the team leader and other core team members. Is the intent to win at any cost or to be a good citizen of the company and operate according to a Looking Glass Culture even if it means losing the business? Or, is it to win by doing what's right for the client and supplier? And, if this is the case, does the team lead have the conviction and courage to effectively manage internal cultural opposition and external competitors?

By "**meaning**," we're talking about the business significance or value of the deal to the client and supplier, as well as, the personal significance to client stakeholders and the pursuit team members.

Lastly, by "**direction**," we mean the ability to know, at any time on any issue, what is directionally correct to winning and what is not accretive to winning with particular emphasis on that which will make or break client and supplier value. That is, we consider the competition and how to defeat them not just based on what is being sold, but how it's being sold with a strong and effective compete strategy.

In our next chapter you'll hear more about the procurement advisor process and how these advisors act as an extension of the client organization as it relates to an important buy. You'll also be introduced to the significant role of a supplier industry advisor and how these individuals provide both formal and informal value to advance a pursuit. All of this will be pulled together and tied into culture on both the sell and buy side of an important opportunity.

11

Buy-Side and Sell-Side Advisors

"Two are better than one, because they have a good return for their labor: If either of them falls down, one can help the other up."—Ecclesiastes 4:9–10

Large deal pursuit campaigns are important, but do they make for a company growth strategy? Yes, they are the key to seeing culture for what it really is and can be a very critical part of the effort to change culture, as we've talked about earlier, but the truth is that nobody really likes big deals. These very important opportunity pursuits reflect big risk—the risk of losing and the risk of being pulled into a Monkey Dance that could end your sales career with a company. That said, the reward can be high, in terms of company revenue, commission, and status in a Client-Centric Culture. Or, if revenue is not the driver, it might be an opportunity to open up a new market or effectively leverage an acquisition of a new company to create a broader solution set.

Whatever it is, if you understand the political landscape of your company and the right people are aware of your sales accomplishments, your influence and success in the company will grow. This is particularly true if a company Fox is watching your back to keep you out of a Monkey Dance on important pursuits where you can safely work outside of a bad culture. In any case, important deals will almost always be sophisticated with advisors working with both suppliers and clients. That sophistication will conceptually move to simplicity if the pursuit lead and deputy are smart and strong, or to complexity if, for example, management by committee sets in to rule the day.

What this means is that deals are not inherently good or bad based upon size. But people are—it's all about the core pursuit team and the culture they live in during the pursuit. Sure, all deals need to be objectively qualified, but if that gives you a green light, it will be you who will make the pursuit complex or straightforward; not easy, but manageable with wisdom and strength. "Listen to advice and accept discipline, and at the end you will be counted among the wise" (Proverbs 19:20).

What are big deals? In the IT system integrator market space, for example, where technology and innovation continue to play a key enabling and transformation role in any company's growth strategy, large deals were historically considered to be in the $1–3 billion range. Today, they span $50–200 million dollars. While these opportunities represent significant revenue, they also cost a lot to pursue with business development budgets often running above one million dollars. And as you know, they attract a lot of attention internally, putting lots of visibility on the pursuit team and their performance in what is at best a high-risk pursuit. Careers can be made or broken when teams operate in a well-founded, but countercultural pursuit. And often, they are broken and not made. On the buy side, customers may have "technical debt" where they lack internal experience, personnel, and processes to run a sophisticated procurement. Companies are often very capable when it comes to outsourcing IT and staff augmentation but may not have experience with transformation projects that drive the advancement of corporate executive priorities through technology enablement.

Making matters worse, if suppliers are operating in a Looking Glass Culture, they will have little to no interest in understanding the customer's business. Providing thought leadership to assist the client in the buying process, as a true partner, will just not happen. As such, the culture gap and the lack of internal large-scale procurement expertise is leading customers to hire procurement advisors who will bring a structured methodology to the buying process. At that point, the procurement advisor becomes an extension of the customer organization with significant influence, while also "insulating" the client from suppliers.

All of this increases supplier risk as they are dealing with two organizations in a restricted and well-controlled sales environment. And while the procurement advisor may act as a cultural buffer between supplier and client to help bring them together, some suppliers will not be able to resist putting their way of doing business first, perhaps disregarding procurement advisor process rules, and end up getting themselves disqualified. It's also possible that the procurement advisor will have an unspoken preference for certain suppliers that they have worked with in the past creating an intangible source of competitive advantage for them that can go completely unnoticed by other supplier companies.

The point here is that when a procurement advisor comes into the deal, supplier risk generally goes up and manageability of risk goes down—part of the reason that large deals become questionable as a growth strategy. Strategically, you have all the variables of an important and competitive sales campaign and those of different pursuit teams; some of which know what they're doing and some that have not gotten to that point. Admittedly, not many suppliers will walk away from a major opportunity. So, to complete the picture, we need to look at the entire big-deal ecosystem that consists of several types of third-party advisors and what they actually do for buyers and sellers. Then, we'll advance to building a blueprint or archetype for the pursuit of all important and competitive deals of all sizes taking into consideration company culture and how it can be managed to produce more value for clients and less competitive vulnerability for suppliers.

A New Industry

On the client buy side of large deals a new procurement advisor industry has evolved for all the reasons introduced earlier. *That said, the goal of the procurement advisor is not to manage the procurement process. He will do that by default, but his mission is to create significant business value for the buyer who is his client.* That means he will provide thought leadership with innovative thinking, a commitment to understand the client's business, and the ability to deliver not only expected value but also to make unexpected contributions to advancing the business—all in a manner that maps properly into the buyer's culture.

Like the supplier who is dealing with the procurement advisor and client, the procurement advisor is dealing with the buyer and an extended number of suppliers. In the beginning there can be as many as twenty or more suppliers in the running until the first and possibly second down select where suppliers are objectively analyzed and qualified to continue in the bid. The logistics alone is a formidable procurement advisor task. Later in the procurement cycle the number may drop to say seven suppliers after the first down select and then in the second down select to three or possibly just two viable suppliers. It's a process that generally includes:

- Assisting the client in setting clear goals and objectives with a supporting budget
- Managing communication with potential suppliers regarding procurement rules and guidelines
- Issuing RFIs (Request for Information) and RFPs
- Scheduling supplier briefings
- Conducting due diligence sessions to address supplier questions
- Reviewing proposals, case study examples, and references
- Setting up supplier presentations
- Organizing supplier site visits
- Establishing down selection criteria and selection
- Overseeing initial negotiations and legal reviews
- Presenting BAFO (Best And Final Offer)
- Managing the negotiation process
- Making supplier recommendations to the client, and
- Sometimes providing ongoing oversight and management of supplier solution implementation.

Working with a number of procurement advisors over the years both as an industry advisor in the IT space and as part of a supplier pursuit team is Rj Smith. Here, he shares with us an experience where a pursuit team of seventy-five direct and independent individuals, of which he was a part, launched a large deal sales campaign costing $2 million in business development expense over a twelve-month period. Justifying this cost and manpower was a possible five-year contract representing more than $1.1 billion. In Rj's words,

> Several years ago, a large corporation in the forest products business, providing paper and pulp offerings through a vertically integrated company structure that was responsible for everything from tree harvesting and conservation to product production and distribution, looked to outsource a large segment of its IT infrastructure to reduce costs and improve operations. They had just completed several acquisitions as part of their growth strategy and were dealing with a number of disparate IT systems that were not integrated. On top of that, they had a very tight timetable if they were to pull everything together and take market share with new and expanded capabilities that were acquired. All of IT, from the technologies employed to the numerous applications to the network and infrastructure, had to be fully integrated. To manage the buying process and do all this, the company hired a procurement advisor who first conducted a benchmarking exercise where the effectiveness and productivity of the IT areas to be outsourced were fully characterized. In this way, the procurement advisor was able to see where productivity gains could be realized and what would be involved in actually achieving those gains. But for

the pursuit team to fully understand how these productivity gains would physically be realized, they had to bring on Subject Matter Experts (SMEs) in the forest products industry, along with financial and legal specialists to round out their team.

To achieve the desired productivity gains, the procurement advisor then quantified the levels of supplier performance that would be needed. This was reflected in the appropriate SLAs (Service Level Agreements) and SOWs (Statements of Work), which made it possible to construct an RFP that went out to a number of qualified suppliers that the procurement advisor knew were capable of doing the work. These firms were contacted and asked to respond to several questions outlining their experience in the specific IT areas. From that exercise a subset of suppliers was asked to attend a session in which they could demonstrate their expertise in fulfilling the RFP requirements with specific examples. This enabled the procurement advisor to verify that the first down selected suppliers were, in fact, capable of performing to the SOW and SLA requirements. From there:

- Each supplier was invited to attend a due diligence session, giving them the opportunity to ask questions, in order to develop their proposed solutions.
- Following the due diligence sessions, suppliers were asked to present their preliminary solutions, while also responding to client questions. The intent was to collaborate, in order to evolve the solutions, with the actual supplier delivery teams leading the presentations and discussions.

- The next step was a second presentation, similar in structure to the first, to preview what the actual and final solutions would look like. This enabled the procurement advisor to perform a second round of down select.

- For those suppliers asked to move to the next round, site visits were conducted to meet with the actual supplier teams doing the work behind the scenes, some of which were offshore.

- Next, a third down select occurred resulting in two finalist suppliers; one was awarded the contract and the second would serve as a backup should it be necessary.

At that point it was believed that either supplier could do the job, in terms of solution, pricing, and delivery. But one supplier also demonstrated an attention to culture. They listened carefully to understand the personality of the client, what they valued, and how it was evidenced in their operations and relationships with their customers, employees, and vendors. This was then incorporated into the supplier solution in the form of flexibility that had little to do with technology and a lot to do with people. At the end of the day, the client felt a level of comfort with the chosen supplier who was already being viewed as a partner.

This is an example where the procurement advisor ran the buy-side acquisition process with the client's support to ensure that the desired client business value was achieved or exceeded. The advisor also ensured a process that was objective, complete, fair, timely, in line with buyer cultural norms, and largely free of supplier protest risk after a decision was made, which is generally a good practice even in the private sector.

The procurement advisor team is often a mix of individuals with backgrounds in the buyer's industry, procurement process, finance, consulting, sales, and delivery. But at the center of all these disciplines is not just procurement methodology. Every company is different, and every industry is different. For the procurement advisor, just as it is for suppliers, understanding the buyer industry is critical to appreciating the buyer's corporate executive priorities, along with their business and vision, direction, market position, competition, and more.

The Industry Advisor

On the sell side, the industry advisor is a rare breed, mainly because unlike the procurement advisor, she has both a formal and informal role that goes well beyond providing information on a specific industry. Certainly, she will understand all there is to know about an industry: what it is, what drives it in terms of market dynamics, emerging and existing trends, the major players, and so on. *But her goal is not to provide information. Her mission centers on knowledge, which consists of information and skills to produce increased business value for the client and competitive advantage for the supplier.* The information part of this goes beyond industry to include the specific client company and the procurement advisor. While an industry advisor may be a supplier employee, that's not always the case as many operate as independent contractors.

As such, the industry advisor may have worked with major procurement advisor firms when supporting suppliers on previous opportunity pursuits, providing informal and invaluable back-channel access to them. She often has pre-existing relationships and credibility,

177

which brings us to the skills piece of her knowledge. A good industry advisor will have strong interpersonal skills in the area of conflict resolution. Working in the white space she can informally help to resolve conflict with the client, procurement advisor, or within the supplier organization. The latter being a must have if a supplier Looking Glass Culture is present.

In addition, an industry advisor will typically have a strong sales background and be able to quickly determine what information is key to the pursuit campaign and what is just noise. This ability to filter and prioritize information is often invaluable as the industry advisor informally assists in guiding the pursuit process. That said, Rj notes, "As contractors, not living with the pursuit team and not being a part of the supplier culture, we can sometimes be viewed not only as outsiders, but as competitors. It all depends on the pursuit team leader. If that person is strong, yet humble, and manages the team to keep egos out of the pursuit, all can work. But if that's not the case, we become sub-optimized, as a resource, very quickly."

Going from Good to Great

We've been looking at a good industry advisor. Now, let's examine what makes a *great* industry advisor. An exceptional industry advisor is one who goes beyond helping to resolve conflict after the fact but also works to resolve conflict before it ever happens. Operationally, this occurs when the industry advisor proactively ensures proper internal alignment within the supplier organization, between supplier and client, and between the supplier and the procurement advisor. It's all about keeping the pursuit team out of a Monkey Dance:

Going from good to great,
Is getting ahead of the Dance.
For when it's too late,
The team has little chance. .

Alignment within the Supplier Organization. Previously, we introduced the industry advisor role and touched upon how she can work within the supplier white space to help reduce the conflict that will exist when a Looking Glass Culture is present. We talked about the Monkey Dance and the role of the executive sponsor in resolving culture conflict that could seriously damage a pursuit campaign. In our example, we had the pursuit lead securing the help of the executive sponsor, which is certainly a viable approach. But a more viable and politically safer approach for the pursuit lead is to have the industry advisor contact the executive sponsor. This tends to depersonalize the situation, as again, the industry advisor is generally not a supplier employee. *She can broker compromises, contain situations dangerous to the pursuit effort, allow people to vent, escalate problems without fear of damaging her career with the supplier company, and protect the integrity and effectiveness of the pursuit lead.*

But, here's the problem: independent industry advisors can easily be discounted by some pursuit team members, as Rj mentioned earlier. We see this when they are not always included in key meetings or client events. An approach to addressing this issue is to increase the authority and influence of the industry advisor, perhaps making her the deputy pursuit lead. Another is to have the powerful executive sponsor acknowledge the role and importance of the industry advisor with the pursuit team. Within the pursuit team there will be a situational Power

Base. It is critical that the industry advisor, along with the pursuit lead and executive sponsor, be in that Power Base. According to Rj, "An important, but informal part of the industry advisor role can be to resolve conflict within the team or between the team and senior management. To do this the industry advisor either needs authority from the assigned position or influence by association with a supplier senior executive."

Alignment between Supplier and Client. The industry advisor will likely know the client, as she is constantly staying in touch with industry leaders, building relationships, and doing research to stay on top of events and trends. These pre-existing relationships are key to avoiding and resolving conflict. They are based upon credibility, trust, and the emphasis that industry advisors place on providing increased value to clients. Again, this is true if the industry advisor is part of the pursuit Power Base. But perhaps an even more important aspect of supplier–client alignment is achieved before the opportunity actually becomes a reality and an RFI or RFP is issued.

Pre-existing industry advisor relationships suggest the possibility of the industry advisor being aware of a potentially major buy taking place in the future. This advanced insight can trigger a pursuit campaign early on before a structured procurement process is put in place and before an RFP is issued, providing an opportunity to shape or pre-wire the RFP and to begin building key client relationships. This creates significant sales momentum before competitors even become aware of the deal. It also provides the supplier with an ability to create demand through thought leadership, often expanding the client requirements to provide unexpected business value that is tied to a corporate executive priority. Providing this type of consultative guidance can not only provide the client with new growth potential, but also expand the deal size, shorten the sales cycle, and dramatically increase the probability of winning the business, which can sometimes be sole sourced.

From Rj's point of view, "It's all about relationships. If the supplier effectively utilizes the industry advisor, that person will be motivated to give that supplier a heads up on new major acquisitions. Without that, or putting an industry advisor on retainer, the supplier may lose the opportunity to launch a sales campaign before the competition even knows about it."

Alignment between Supplier and Procurement Advisor. The moment that a supplier is down selected based upon the recommendation of the procurement advisor, it's critical that the supplier demonstrate the behavior and attributes that advance cultural alignment with the client. How business value is provided can be as important as the value itself. To accomplish this, the procurement advisor conceptually acts as a cultural buffer with the operational requirement of having an inside industry advisor supporter within the supplier organization to drive compliance from within. This augments the forced compliance that the procurement advisor can dictate, but that cannot be solely depended on, as too much use of "force" or authority creates attitudinal problems that will surface in other ways at other times. As such, the industry advisor is key to the implementation of the principle that dictates economy of force, which is the minimum use of procurement advisor authority to resolve a problem with careful and effective escalation when necessary, often in the judgment of the industry advisor.

Rj comments, "During one important pursuit that I was involved in, the pursuit team decided to discount the importance of specific RFP requirements as the supplier did not have a strong solution in that area, as compared to the competition. Then, during one of the customer meetings, where the pursuit team lead was presenting, the customer and procurement advisor took notice of it, which resulted in both of them feeling that the supplier did not read the RFP. This not only challenged their professionalism, but also signaled a lack of caring, which was clearly a reflection of supplier sales culture. This type of thing happens, and when it does, the situation will go one of two ways: either the procurement advisor will use his authority and disqualify the supplier or its team members, or the procurement advisor will informally work with the industry advisor to correct the situation from the inside out. Due to the sensitivity of this particular situation, I won't comment further, but you can see how diplomacy with an industry advisor insider can guide and fix supplier problems to build even stronger relationships going forward."

Summary of Chapter 11

In this chapter, you were introduced to the procurement advisor whose mission is not to manage the procurement process, but to create significant business value for the client through a structured procurement process. To accomplish this, you've seen their role in action, as we have outlined the general methodology employed within that industry. You've also been introduced to the formal and informal role of the industry specialist who works on the sell side of a deal with suppliers. For them, the goal is not just to provide information; their mission centers on knowledge—which consists of information *and* skills—powerful and thorough enough to drive increased business value for the client and competitive advantage for the supplier.

As you can see, both the procurement and industry advisors' focus, first and foremost, is on providing client value, which puts them at odds with a supplier Looking Glass Culture and the internal focus that it drives. That said, it places the industry advisor in a great position to assist a pursuit team lead in not only resolving conflict, like that of a Monkey Dance, but also resolving conflict before it actually materializes. The ability to work effectively in the white space of an organization is the hallmark of an independent industry advisor. This applies to working issues within the supplier organization, between the supplier and the client, and between the supplier and the procurement advisor.

In the next and last chapter, we'll advance the discussion of advisors on the sell side to include campaign advisors who assist in winning business, while strengthening pursuit teams and culture. And we'll wrap up the chapter series with seven critical thinking points that characterize a successful pursuit campaign for important opportunities.

12

Sell-Side Support

"Blessed are those who find wisdom, those who gain understanding, for she is more profitable than silver and yields better returns than gold."—Proverbs 3:13–14

On the sell side with suppliers who demonstrate either Client-Centric or Confused Cultures the opportunity exists for a campaign advisor team to assist in securing an important and competitive opportunity. *That said, the goal is not to win the deal, but to win the battle and grow in strength. The mission is to win the business, build team expertise, and strengthen culture.* Winning is important, but more important is to build up supplier teams and culture, as assets, to win future opportunities in the absence of campaign advisors. This is accomplished by guiding the pursuit team; working closely with the team core that includes the pursuit lead and deputy/industry advisor, and the executive sponsor. This guidance operates in accordance with a blueprint to produce a supplier-specific archetype or guidebook for future and important pursuit campaigns of all sizes.

On occasion, the campaign advisor may work within a Looking Glass Culture if a supplier effort is being made to improve the company culture. That notwithstanding, working within a Looking Glass Culture is generally futile. While there are exceptions, a lack of proper pursuit team configuration, along with cultural preoccupation, inward focus, lack of client insight, and little desire to improve, make nearly all important and competitive opportunity pursuits little more than an exercise in rolling the dice with lots of frustration along the way.

When campaign advisor support does make sense, it involves their doing research into the client's business and the supplier's competition to augment the industry advisor's efforts. From there, heavy focus is placed on qualifying the opportunity and identifying missing information to be certain that the business development expense is justified.

This then leads to the development of a sales campaign that dovetails into the client procurement cycle, as mentioned in the last chapter, including taking full advantage of early entry when possible. This will include crafting a pursuit team mission statement, determining client-centric value positioning, aligning with the client political landscape, developing a compete strategy, and focusing heavily on tactical implementation. Particular emphasis should be placed on client-facing and sales-supporting activities, such as generating proposals, conducting presentations, and negotiating with the client.

All major client-facing activities are continually tested against the pursuit mission and strategy to first ensure down select. Post down select, a reanalysis takes place, as the competitive deck is reshuffled with a likely new competitive landscape. New value positioning is often required to defeat a potentially new primary competitor. At the same time, coaching of the pursuit team is taking place to increase their capability and capacity, and codify the campaign approach into a supplier-specific roadmap for future sales engagements. Simultaneously, and in the supplier background, the campaign advisor and core pursuit team are working to manage and resolve any cultural conflict that might exist based upon cultural alignment with the client and procurement advisor.

This campaign advisor backend work is as important as the front-facing sales work, as "a house divided against itself cannot stand" (Abraham Lincoln). A pursuit team cannot "fight" on two fronts. It must be unified, and it must also be compatible with the buy-side client culture, which is also emphasized in Mark 3:25, "If a house is divided against itself, that house cannot stand."

When adversity arises, either within a pursuit team or between the team and supplier management, pressurizing the environment with strong differences of opinion, division will quickly devolve into derision, creating an emotionally charged situation. "No one can serve two masters; for either he will hate the one and love the other, or he will be devoted to one and despise the other" (Matthew 6:24). But this doesn't mean that the pursuit team or supplier company should lose its identity or try to be something that it's not; rather it reflects the need to align with the buy-side culture relative to beliefs, values, morals, and ethics that relate specifically to the sales campaign and solution being sold, along with its implementation. The intent is not only to achieve smooth sales operations, but to create a nontraditional source of competitive advantage. The expertise behind this intent can be viewed in terms of critical thinking that relates to the pursuit of very important opportunities.

Seven Critical Thinking Points

"Critical thinking is self-directed, self-disciplined, self-monitored, and self-corrective thinking. It presupposes assent to rigorous standards of excellence and mindful command of their use. It entails effective communication and problem-solving abilities as well as a commitment to overcome native egocentrism and sociocentrism."[1] And all this takes place with subtext, which translates into cultural influences, spoken and unspoken. For this reason and to assist you in going forward with important deal pursuits, the following seven critical thinking points are offered. They are limited to essential information only designed to direct and guide at a strategic level.

1. **Define Important.** Important deals are almost always highly competitive. What's of interest to you will likely be of interest to your competition. High revenue value is a no-brainer. But what about other circumstances? For example, new innovation. By definition, you may not have an installed base to serve as sales references. This makes credibility an issue, particularly if the new offering is disruptive to legacy practices and thinking, or disruptive to existing client culture. This is particularly true if the new technology is outside the supplier's core business that has historically fueled its growth. Bill McDermott, when he was CEO of SAP, once told us that to sell offerings outside of ERP (Enterprise Resource Planning), SAP often had to go through a proof-of-concept phase for an ERP adjunctive solution. In another case, "important" may

---

1 en.wikipedia.org/wiki/Critical_thinking

be reflected in an opportunity within a smaller company that doesn't represent a lot of revenue. But the client may be part of a large international firm where your company has no installed base. As such, the deal could serve as a "foot in the door" of a new account. And therefore, it is important. Or, an opportunity in a particular quarter might make the difference in making quota. Whatever the reason, resist the thinking that all deals are important and realize that they are not all created equally. Depending on circumstances, some will be more important than others.

2. **Identify Potential.** Identify the companies and industries that have the potential to support important opportunities in your region or district. Establish a relationship with a local industry advisor for each of the key industries if possible, or work with other sales regions to utilize and have access to their industry advisor resources. The industry advisor will be able to identify emerging trends and shifts in company business models that could produce new opportunities going forward. For example, if you're in the technology services business, be on the lookout for companies implementing or planning to implement the growth strategy introduced earlier in this book, as it requires digital transformation and cost reduction that could represent significant opportunity.

3. **Get in Early.** Focus on winning the battle before it's fought. Working with the appropriate industry advisor, secure any advance notice or indications of future important opportunities that may develop. Then launch an exploratory sales

campaign wherever it makes sense, in order to get in before the competition and before the client's thinking has solidified. At that point, your thought leadership and that of the industry advisor can potentially shape the opportunity. In the United States, federal government acquisitions take place under FAR (Federal Acquisition Regulation) that impose a very structured procurement process producing a very restrictive selling environment. During this period, deals can be lost, but not really won. Winning happens when the stage has been set to win before FAR kicks in, which is why the pre-FAR period sales effort is referred to as Business Development and the post-FAR period is considered Bid Management. You'll find that every day you're early in, ahead of the competition, your competitive advantage increases. Sometimes, very dramatically. Supporting this increase is early value alignment. That is your ability to map into a client value chain that starts at the top of the customer organization, in the form of corporate executive priorities. An example is a recent CNBC interview with the CEO of Starbucks, Kevin Johnson, where he said, "The more digital relationships we have the better. I mean it is the number one most powerful thing we can do in the United States to drive same store growth. . . . We're now at 20 million digitally registered customers."[2] Your goal is to advance an executive priority by first identifying what parts of the customer organization have various responsibilities relating to it.

---

2 www.cnbc.com/video/2018/06/20/watch-cnbcs-full-exclusive-interview-with-starbucks-ceo-kevin-johnson.html

In the case of Starbucks, perhaps it's a group in marketing, store operations, and IT. These are customer areas that you can view as value chain, each working to advance the executive priority in specific ways. And, you can be assured that each is well funded with budget to do the job. Plus, with focus on the executive priority, you've always got an audience.

4. **Go or No Go**. Qualify the potential opportunity. Does it quantifiably make sense to pursue based on the qualification score? Using the same qualification criteria, determine what level of effort and cost will be involved in the pursuit. You will find that you're missing key information. Go out and get it and make certain that you have reasonable proof statements from the client that support a good rational for scoring each qualification criterion. That doesn't mean that you need a crystal ball, but it does suggest that you should not take anything from the client at face value. Once done, identify the necessary resources required to drive the sales campaign and verify that they are available or can be acquired in a timely manner.

5. **Team Up**. Configure the pursuit team and establish the necessary setup to ensure that it can operate effectively. The team size can be as small as the team lead, industry advisor, and executive sponsor on limited but important pursuits. If your company is operating under a Looking Glass or Confused Culture, be certain to have the right executive sponsor and industry advisor who are willing and able to play a nontraditional role in resolving cultural conflict. If you sense cultural

conflict, know that your wings are on fire. You must avoid a Monkey Dance whenever possible by anticipating and resolving cultural problems before they fully develop. You can't win business, grow in strength, and be worried about protecting your career at the same time.

6. **Close the Deal.** When an important sales campaign is peaking and a decision is about to be made, explicitly close. Don't seek comfort waiting for the client to call you or massage the situation to gently move the client to a decision. Meet face-to-face and ask for the order in any manner that is consistent with your personal style. This is a time when you must demonstrate an offensive vs. defensive mindset. Fear of rejection needs to be put out of your mind. So, be direct. The worst that can happen is a trial close that will surface any concerns or issues that the client may have in going with you. This is a time for conviction and spirit:

It's the moment of truth,

When closing a deal.

Like that time in your youth,

When you moved with zeal.

7. **Seek Wisdom.** Critical and often elusive, wisdom is "the ability or result of an ability to think and act utilizing knowledge, experience, understanding, common sense, and insight."[3] And when it comes to this ability, we are all on a learning curve that our sales performance is tied to—with only one way to really

---

3 www.thefreedictionary.com/wisdom

compensate for it: to borrow the right wisdom, at the right time, and apply it in the right way. That's a lot of "rights" and so our best advice is to reduce them to just one right, one that is very fundamental and reliable, as it is based upon absolute truth. It won't be sales specific, but as you're likely experienced in sales, you'll figure out how to apply it, as Proverbs 1:5 says, "Let the wise listen and add to their learning, and let the discerning get guidance." *We recommend that during the few quiet moments that you contemplate pursuing a new and important sales opportunity, you open your Bible or download a Bible app to your phone and turn to Proverbs. And just start reading. The wisdom you need will find you, for, "Ask and it will be given to you; seek and you will find; knock and the door will be opened to you" (Matthew 7:7).*

Summary of Chapter 12

In this last chapter, you've been introduced to the campaign advisor who carries the mission of assisting a pursuit team in winning a specific piece of business, while building team expertise and strengthening sales culture to help win future important deals. In addition, you have seen seven critical thinking points that are highly material to winning important opportunities, particularly in bad supplier cultures. They are limited to essential information only, designed to guide and protect you when working in a Looking Glass Culture or working with egocentric personalities. They are a form of packaged wisdom, presented at a strategic level and intended for both heart and mind.

Epilogue

As you know, this is a book about declining sales effectiveness and its connection to culture, conflict, and anxiety. It's about how sales effectiveness—evidenced by the moments of truth that observant sellers experience in working with clients—shines a light on supplier culture, showing it to be good or bad, and how the conflict of a Looking Glass Culture and doing what is right for clients can create personal and professional risk for sellers. This risk engenders fear that results in anxiety as sellers face career risk on one side and losing deals on the other. At the same time, clients are basically in the same boat where personal and professional risk are top of mind in significant buys, as gig culture has given rise to Looking Glass Cultures in so many companies, market sectors, and countries. That puts risk, fear, and anxiety on both sides of a significant deal with the seller in the middle. As a result, characterizing culture to better understand and manage it is really what this book is about.

This has required us to go beyond simply conveying information and insight—as would characterize a traditional business book—to include the element of emotion. We could not write about anxiety without it. This is why we have included a bit of poetry, along with personal examples and those from other domains—like mountaineering and dealing with adversaries in a law enforcement or counterterrorism role, or cancer for that matter. These domains involve people confronting danger in emotionally charged situations.

Historically, the business risk in selling has always been something that everyone understood, accepted, and managed. But, that's not true today. The gig culture and other factors that we've discussed in this book have brought a new kind of perceived risk into large-ticket sales. And although it's not physical risk, it's easily internalized and can be deeply disturbing.

Selling and Mountaineering Emotion

If you are a sales manager or an executive, think of yourself as a seller for a moment, imagine that you're climbing a mountain that symbolizes the relationship with your customer. You've qualified the mountain in that conditions are good for the ascent from base camp, just as you would qualify an important opportunity. But unlike selling, if you make a mistake, you could die. On all but one of my climbs on Mount Rainier, they were preceded or followed by bodies being taken off the mountain. So, you begin your climb and make camp at the base of the upper mountain, which is steeper, harder, and way more dangerous than your climb so far on the lower mountain.

But, you're there, just as is the case in being down selected on a key pursuit. In both cases the deck gets reshuffled with changing weather on the mountain and changes in the competitive landscape post down select. At sunup you awake with hot tea, stretch, and get ready to climb, while also keeping a watchful eye on the weather and mountain conditions. It's like checking to see if your primary competitor in the sales pursuit post down select is the same as the one at pre down select—as the customer has gone from twelve potential suppliers to three—while also keeping a watchful eye on whether you're number one, two, or three in competitive position.

The climb is now steep and dangerous as you move up the white icy glacier that gravity has pulled apart to form deep crevasses that run thirty to forty feet deep with running water under them. Across these crevasses are narrow snow bridges that can collapse at any moment. At the same time, you're roped to your teammates as you zig zag up the glacier, crossing the snow bridges. You walk in the exact footsteps of the climber ahead of you, as he has not fallen into the crevasse. If you do break through a snow bridge, you yell, "Falling!" and spread your arms out wide to, hopefully, fall only up to your neck and stop. Everyone self-arrests by diving into the glacier with ice ax in one hand, ice hammer in the other, and burying the two front points of their twelve-point crampons on each foot into the ice. But, if you break through the snow bridge and fall, it will be to the distance of the slack in your line, as will be the severity of your headache when the rope goes taught at altitude—or worse, if you hit a ledge in the crevasse. Next, is crevasse rescue by your team to get you out and back into the climb . . . if you're not hurt too much. But all this will depend on how well the team is prepared to do the rescue, setting up pulleys if necessary and providing medical support. If you're not prepared, it's like experiencing the excitement of being down selected and believing that all you have to do to win is more of what you did earlier, but then finding out that your primary competitor has changed, your value positioning is too generic, and your key supporter is not in the Power Base.

You've now been climbing for hours; fifty minutes on and then stopping to rest for ten minutes, each hour. You're sweating heavily for those fifty minutes and when you stop, you freeze. So, you quickly pull your heavy parka out from your backpack and throw it on to stay warm while resting and drinking water. As you look up, you see a wall of ice and rock. It's an acute vertical and you will need to cross it. The ledge is about thirty feet long and just six inches wide. But that's not the real problem.

Above you, there are hundreds of feet of loose ice and rock that can fall right where you'll be crossing. Your heart rate builds, and your breath gets shorter as you approach it and begin to see down hundreds of feet where rock and blocks of ice have fallen and landed, crashing into the mountain below. Falling in the crevasse was scary, but this objective hazard brings on real fear. You can do everything right and still die. It's where your ego gets checked before proceeding.

Strong and successful but egocentric people will often go no further as they see themselves for who they really are with bravado masking insecurity. It's like what a Looking Glass Culture can make people believe, in terms of what's right, when it's really wrong. It's no different than the moments of truth seen by a seller. On a mountain, the truth cannot be hidden. That said, you get through it and continue climbing to high camp, which you must reach before sundown. Getting there, you power down, drink lots of water, eat, and rest in your sleeping bag. Midnight will come soon, and with it, your assault on the summit.

It's dark, cold, and the way is steep. You wonder if the battery powering the light that's attached to your helmet will keep its power in the cold thin air above you. Nobody talks much. Everyone looks around constantly, hypersensitive to changing mountain conditions, and trying to memorize landmarks that could mean life or death if a rapid descent is required. You move with careful hurry to reach the summit safely in about eleven hours, but you feel anxiety for hours until the sun rises. Then, the dissonance turns to pure excitement. Now, the higher you go, the better you feel with the warm sun powering you forward. Finally, you reach the summit hoping that clouds will not block the view. Again, no one talks, everyone just takes it in, as it is literally and figuratively a breathtaking panorama of blue sky and mountains.

Every time I climbed Mount Rainier in the late 1980s, I was in awe looking at the self-destructive state of Mount St. Helens that had gone through so much eruptive activity. Reaching the summit safely is an emotional high that makes you feel like you're nineteen years old, and it's legal—not unlike winning a super important deal with the team support of a Client-Centric Culture that becomes everyone's win. That's joy in selling.

One could argue that confronting any significant challenge in life with truth, honor, and dignity—independent of outcome—is real joy.

Quick Reference

This Quick Reference provides fast access to important concepts, ideas, and guidance rather than the traditional word indexing that's typical with business books. The intent is to make for a great reader experience that's quick, productive, and engaging:

Subject	Content
Value for Sellers *Page xxxvi*	This book is for sellers who not only want to be successful and build a career, but also desire quality of life and want to be able to enjoy their work. It's about recognizing and navigating the incredible anxiety your buyers and decision-makers are feeling, while also recognizing your own anxiety that could have you drifting into an inward company focus to cope with that anxiety.
Value for Sales Managers *Page xxxvii*	This book is also for sales managers and company executives who see and recognize the decline in sales effectiveness today and want to understand and better manage how culture-induced anxiety is damaging productivity, innovation, and the customer centricity that is at the heart of profitable

Subject	Content
Continued from previous page	growth. In many companies, pipeline volume is shrinking, velocity in the pipe is down, sales forecasting is becoming less and less accurate, win rates are decreasing, and while some large companies are market leaders, they are not growing as they should. *Sales managers can immediately help sellers drive business by reducing the noise that they have to deal with each and every day to free up time*—that is, time to research and better prepare for customer calls, proposals, and presentations. As a simple example, in today's company culture, five superficial sales calls per week are more valued than two with substance. This must change.
Value for Company Executives *Page xxxviii*	Company executives can also play a key role. For those firms that want to seriously improve Customer Experience, this book will provide a diagnostic that can be run to characterize and define company culture. *You will see the culture that the executive team believes exists and be able to compare it to the actual culture that sellers know to be true, as they directly deal with its impact on sales that makes it very visible to them.* Seeing the gap between the two is strategically invaluable.

Subject	Content
Merging Creativity and Intellect Poem *Page xl*	*This is business redefined,* *To give what can't be bought.* *It's art and logic combined,* *To feel the power of thought.*
Generic Sales Messaging *Page 7*	"'The presentation looked very similar to one the consulting firm had given previously to another business unit within Puma,' he adds. *'There were 80 slides full of prophecies and bubbles,'* Mr. Hassenstein says. 'I was confused, and it was a very deterring experience.'"
Not Knowing Customers *Page 7, 8*	In an age of nearly instantaneous access to copious amounts of information, sellers have never had less insight into their customer base. *In an age of hyperconnectivity, it's easy to communicate and easier to communicate ineffectively due to distraction and lack of time.* "Beware the barrenness of a busy life," said Socrates.
Working and Living in a Culture without Adopting its Values *Page 16*	The Bible, however, takes a different approach. It doesn't seek to define culture, but rather to focus on the acceptability of culture. *It acknowledges that people need to be in the world, but at the same time, don't need to be controlled by the world.* Independent of your religious views, this useful piece of instruction indicates that one should not simply conform to a culture.

Subject	Content
Company Culture Assessment *Page 21-27*	What Culture Are You Living In? And identifying the three types of company culture: • Client-Centric Culture • Looking Glass Culture • Confused Culture
Culture Gap Between the Executive and Field Sales Views *Page 27*	It's knowing what you value, your company values, and what your customers value, and how they all play together. To help with this, you now have a diagnostic to differentiate good from bad culture with the latter driving a strong inward company focus that is insensitive to clients and winning business. Your executive leadership also has the ability to look at your company's culture in terms of what they want it to be and what it really is, which is the first step to building it up and providing customers with enhanced CX.
Influence and Authority *Page 29*	It's true that company founders set the acceptable mindset and behaviors within a startup, often based upon their personal values, and that company executives have the power to initiate and support cultural change. *But that said, all organizations will eventually adopt a type of collective control of their culture, independent of authority and very much driven by influence.* This recognizes that influence and authority are not synonymous.

Subject	Content
Continued from previous page *Page 57*	Cultural change is all about leadership, requiring political power, timing, and entrepreneurial ability. And this begins with mapping out your company's political landscape to create a support base for cultural change, just as you would do in accounts to win important deals.
Client-Centric Culture *Page 40*	To really create a Client-Centric Culture the sellers will need to develop a heartfelt respect for clients that reflects a high level of sensitivity toward them to the extent of being able to put themselves in the shoes of the clients, where empathy resides. It's a sensitivity that acknowledges that clients live with risk, as well, and that everything possible needs to be done to help them reduce that risk as it relates to your business. It's listening carefully and being both intellectually and emotionally committed to assisting them.
Cultural Sensitivity and Humility Climbing Example *Page 40, 41*	I had the good fortune to climb Mount Rainier a number of times. As I was first training on Nisqually Glacier for a week with Phil Ershler, an accomplished mountain climber and trainer, I began to develop my climbing philosophy. Somewhat similar to culture, it consisted of a set

Subject	Content
Continued from previous page	of principles to follow for high altitude technical mountaineering. These principles include: • When in doubt chicken out. One of the first things Phil told me early on was that there is nothing romantic about dying on a mountain. • Speed is safety. For me and my climbing team that meant not just moving fast but moving to safety. • No bivouac equipment. I believed that if you don't have it, you can't use it. Therefore, we needed the best possible situational awareness of weather and mountain conditions, which meant knowing the mountain. But to make this philosophy operational and effective, required: • *Sensitivity*, listening and watching everything, from looking back to know the way down to safety, to watching the freeze point as an indicator of avalanche potential, to signs of storm fronts, to listening to our bodies for physical and emotional issues. *Translation: Listen to the customer with sincerity to not only hear and understand what they need and are saying, but to know their culture and the values that define the company.*

Subject	Content
Continued from previous page	• *Humility*, knowing that the mountain is king. It calls the shots. There is no place for ego on a mountain, no matter how successful or great you think you are—the mountain rules. *Translation: Respectfully recognize the authority of the customer.*
Why Culture Change Begins in Sales *Page 45-53*	What is the compelling argument for cultural change to operationally begin in the sales organization? There are five reasons why sellers are in the perfect position to effect change: • Proximity, Value, and Relevance • Face-to-Face Client Time • Access to Resources • Being Relevant • Discerning the Political Landscape
Having Conviction and Boldness to Put Clients First *Page 47*	This means that sellers and sales managers need to be strong and persistent, demonstrating conviction and boldness. Conviction is believing in the absence of proof, as evidenced by your actions. But believing that customers should come first is one thing. It's another to go against the culture and perhaps against your senior management . . . maybe even putting your job on the line. Risk averse people simply will not do it. But even those who will, need the strength of

Subject	Content
Continued from *previous page*	their convictions. They need to be bold. *If conviction is believing in the absence of proof, as evidenced by your actions, conviction and boldness together is believing in the absence of proof, as evidenced by your actions irrevocably.*
Believing in **Clients Poem** *Page 49*	*From where does the belief come,* *And where does the boldness lie?* *With trust they move as one,* *Like birds together they fly.*
The Power **Base** *Page 59*	When we think about organizational politics, we view it as a Power Base, the influential body within an organization. Think of this group as a social network sitting on a professional platform. It is made up of influential people who communicate frequently and who share common values. As such, it is not only a power-ful network of people, but also one with its own subculture that tends to shape the environment around it. Unlike an organization chart that clearly and tangibly identifies individuals, their positions, and level of authority, the Power Base is not visible and only becomes so when its members are exerting influence, particularly across department lines in areas where the Power Base members have no authority.

Subject	Content
Continued from previous page	*In a Power Base, there is no formal component to the social order, only that of influence and culture where the culture provides stability and influence provides power.*
Foxes *Page 59-65*	Leadership resides with one person whom we symbolize as a Fox. This person is the center of influence and all others in the Power Base derive their power by association with him or her. Foxes are not like most people. They are not easy to spot unless you know very well what to look for in an organization.
	Foxes are an asset to any company in that they provide both formal and informal leadership throughout an organization with a minimum of bureaucracy, which is particularly important when formal leadership channels get bogged down. So, what do we know about Foxes, in terms of descriptive traits? • Results Oriented • Situationally Aware • Able to Work in Exception to Policy • Calculated Risk Takers • Strong Delegators • Great Listeners • Humble • Change Agents

Subject	Content
Jackals *Page 60, 61*	Foxes put their companies first, ahead of themselves, and never work to advance themselves at the expense of their companies. A Jackal, on the other hand, looks like a Fox but is not. He is a scavenger and a very different animal. In a company, when you spot a very powerful individual with strong influence, but also with a willingness to advance his or her own interests at the expense of the company, he is not a Fox, but a Jackal. And, if there is one thing we can say about corporate Jackals, it is to stay far away from them.
Jackal Poem *Page 62*	The people who engage in such activity don't wear black hats or hooded sweatshirts. On the contrary, they suit up well and look like Foxes, but are manipulative in nature. They are Jackals. *Beware, beware,* *Looks can deceive.* *What will appear,* *Is not to believe.*
Types of Power Bases *Page 68*	There are two types of Power Bases: organizational and situational. Every company business unit, division, and department will have an organizational Power Base, and in addition, there will be a corporate executive Power Base at the

Subject	Content
Continued from previous page	top of the organization. Generally speaking, these Power Bases reside within, and are defined by, the organizational scope of their group and are often quite stable. A situational Power Base, on the other hand, is created when something important is occurring. It may be a major procurement, a restructuring of the business, or perhaps a contemplated buy, sell, or merger.
Moments of Truth *Page 70*	There is a time when a Looking Glass Culture can no longer be tolerated by high performing sellers. This occurs when a moment of truth emerges, a time when the presence of a Looking Glass Culture is about to destroy a qualified and important pursuit. Yellow flashing warning signs emerge at the customer interface, as your sales culture finds the following to be acceptable and expected: • Generic proposals and presentations, often part of a unified messaging effort • A lack of clear understanding of the customer's business, such as their vision, direction, and priorities • Value that is not positioned to advance customer executive priorities either directly or indirectly, perhaps focused on operational value and cost reduction

Subject	Content
Continued from previous page	• Political alignment that really doesn't exist, such as when a friendly supporter is mistaken to be the situational Fox • The pursuit team is leading by committee.
Entrepreneurship Page 72	The word *entrepreneur* is French, meaning one who undertakes a task that involves initiative and risk. And, as the catalyst for cultural change, you will need lots of initiative and will be taking on lots of risk. As we've said before, a culture will resist change, destroying or purging itself of anything it can't conform to itself or assimilate. Any culture will resist change with the power of a freight train. Its inertia is strong; its will even stronger. Get in its way and the outcome is certain. But surgically narrow your focus to the cultural Power Base, as in the track ahead, and you can derail bad culture.
Charlie Kirk and College Culture that's Shaping the Future Workforce *Page 81*	"If we view academic culture as a living, breathing organism and conceptually drop it into a company today that has built and supports a Client-Centric Culture, which is also considered a living entity, the one will destroy the other."

Subject	Content
The Science of Caring *Page 91*	Let's look at culture where CX or Customer Experience is driven by the level of caring for customers and also apply it to employees within a company. Here, caring momentum is also subject to the law of conservation of momentum, as there is only so much of it available within an organization—and within an individual.
Culture Normalizes the Irrational *Page 97*	You can't touch the moments of truth that signal a Looking Glass Culture, but with the right focus and mindset you can recognize what's happening. You can see the consequences of lost business clearly enough to know that something is wrong, even though the culture will attempt to normalize the irrational to a point where it appears rational.
Anxiety *Page 102, 103*	Psychologists tell us that internalized fear, regret, or guilt are things that people can easily begin to ruminate or become fixated on; reflecting on something over and over again. When that happens a person's imagination can kick in creating images of a worst-case situation. For example, say you're working in a counterculture manner, not following accepted cultural norms, in order to secure an important piece of business. That is, the sales campaign requires you to propose X,

Subject	Content
Continued from previous page	but a powerful person in your company wants you to propose Y because it's important to your company's growth plan. Also assume that going against the wishes of the executive could potentially put your job at risk and going against what the customer needs and expects could put the deal at risk. And so, you begin to imagine all the bad things that could happen by not following the executive directive; professionally, economically, and at home, if you lose your position. As the brain and unconscious mind has no ability to differentiate between imagination and reality,[1] perceived risk develops into fear and then physiologically into anxiety. Then, when that anxiety gets too high and surpasses the fear of losing a deal, you think twice about proposing X. After all, clients will come and go, but you will continue to live with the people in your company. People who can advance or inhibit your career. Is the risk of a sales loss greater than that of a career loss?
Personification of Culture *112, 113*	Cultures are made up of people, with each culture consisting of a unique matrix of human qualities that are interdependent and interrelated in such a way as to form a "living" entity, one that can

---

1 Reference: drdavidhamilton.com/does-your-brain-distinguish-real-from-imaginary/

Subject	Content
Continued from previous page	exert influence, for one purpose: to shape human behavior in very specific ways and to do so with scale. *To see culture is to know it.* More specifically, to see it as a person, an intelligent life form, is to know it. Personification of a sophisticated entity, like culture that is made up of its cultural inhabitants, drives a more holistic view, including all of its human-like character- istics, and does so with observable depth. That makes culture "someone" that can draw power from very specific sources and use it to adapt and protect itself for good or for bad. Go against it and you will most likely become frustrated and fail or leave. That said, it's not invincible if you think outside the box and don't take it on directly with the traditional methods of legislation, policy, and even compensation.
Personifying Cancer with the Zuza Story *Page 120-123*	Zuza was a small black kitten left at the doorstep of a veterinarian when we adopted him. He was named after a silver back gorilla that I helped hand rear at Brookfield Zoo outside of Chicago. "Zuza" means "gift" in Swahili. . . *Personifying cancer, just as with company culture, showed it to be strategic, intelligent, and strong.*

Subject	Content
Culture Strengthens Itself and Culture Change Poem *Page 124*	For that reason, a Client-Centric Culture or Looking Glass Culture will actively attract people who share its values and work to promote those people into positions of power, sometimes independent of their performance. In this regard, a bad culture becomes worse, while a good culture sustains itself. *It also means that the time required to damage a culture is short, while the time to repair it is long:* *Good or bad or not,* *Culture is strong.* *But time to damage is short,* *While time to heal is long.*
Potentiation *Page 124, 125*	The cancer dynamic created by the partnership between myeloma and bone marrow stromal cells not only drives rapid growth of the cancer, but also makes it immortal. In culture, the strength and longevity of its traditional norms is determined by the potentiation of people and time.
***Titanic* Example of Potentiation** *Page 127, 128*	Perhaps one of the most dramatic examples of potentiation is the sinking of the *Titanic* where the coming together or confluence of specific elements combined to potentiate each other and doom the boat. Yet, no one element was really significant. But combined, they tell a different story.

Subject	Content
Looking Glass Culture Potentiation *Page 129-131*	A Looking Glass Culture has a personality that tends to dehumanize customers, discounting and subordinating them to itself. We read a lot today about technology dehumanizing people, but this is only one piece of the puzzle. In addition to people and time potentiating each other within a culture, there are four other factors that fuel the culture dynamic through potentiation: • Intimacy without Engagement • Driven to Distraction • Cultural Preoccupation • Self-entitlement The effect of these four factors is not equal to their sum but is exponentially greater as they reinforce each other to produce disproportionate culture growth, strength, and the ability to resist change. They not only dehumanize clients, but when that happens over a long enough period of time, it is our view that the culture also begins to dehumanize sellers and sales managers, showing little care for their opinions, experience, ability, and career well-being. This is the destructive power and dynamic of a Looking Glass Culture.

Subject	Content
The Pace of Culture Change *Page 132, 133*	The Culture Change Process. *When driving behavioral change in people there is an optimal pace to effect change that is sustainable, just as is the case in nature and society.* The same holds true with culture. The personification of culture provides you with added insight as to who it is and how it operates because it's made up of people. In all these cases, culture, society, and nature, equilibrium needs to be maintained so that the environment will remain stable. But at the same time, change disturbs equilibrium, which results in forces immediately working to restore it. These forces exist as feedback to the change and can achieve stabilization by stopping the change initiative or by institutionalizing the change so that it becomes part of the culture with equilibrium once again restored. *In society, nature, and culture, the resistance to change will directly relate to the magnitude of the change and the speed with which it's being driven.*
Pace of Change Mt. Kilimanjaro Example *Page 134-136*	To look at the pace of change from a team perspective, I'd like to take you back to Mt. Kilimanjaro. My team's approach to the summit was to transverse the mountain over a period of seven days, which would help us acclimate to the

Subject	Content
Continued from previous page	altitude. It began with a steep hike up the rain forest to the Shira Plateau at 10,000 feet, then, across the mountain and up to high camp at Barafu, 15,500 feet. At midnight we made the summit attempt to Uhuru Peak at 19,341 feet, which took eleven hours. On the way, back at the Shira Plateau, we found ourselves climbing in parallel with a German team. We had set up the tents and were preparing for very bad weather that we expected that night when we observed the German team climbing some of the steep verticals in the area. It was impressive, and while we were keeping very busy to both get ready for nightfall and accelerate acclimation to the altitude, we wondered if we should be climbing as well. But something told us not to overdrive so early in the climb. For days this level of activity was the routine of the Germans who were very disciplined, well prepared with good equipment, and in great shape, being strong and athletic. We all thought that these guys would fly to the summit, but fast forward to the approach on Barafu and the German team went missing. It turned out that they had been suffering from headaches, vomiting, dizziness, and extreme fatigue. Moving

Subject	Content
Continued from previous page	too hard and too fast with low oxygen levels had brought on altitude sickness, the number one cause of death on Mt. Kilimanjaro.
The Monkey Dance *Page 143-145*	Remember our primate behavior example where the monkeys in a cage had been behaviorally conditioned? Well, hang on then. When a pursuit team runs into a disagreement with a company individual who is inflicted with cultural preoccupation, they will likely be pushing on some aspect of a Looking Glass Culture. It may be an executive who insists the team take an approach that is counter to the pursuit effort or to what the client requires, or one that is contraindicated to whatever the pursuit team lead feels is required to win the business. This is a strategic problem that has the potential to derail the entire pursuit. It's a situation that occurs, to varying degrees, far more often than you would likely think. And when it happens, the executive is often adamant about it, as he is in a mode of self-deception. Again, this fear-based denial reduces the anxiety of not complying with company culture and what is expected, often induced by career concerns; not putting the company first or not aligning with the views of a very senior and powerful executive.

Subject	Content
Continued from previous page	This is anxiety anesthetized by rationalizing away your team's argument and logic. When this is the case and civil discourse fails, you're in a Monkey Dance. *The desired outcome of a Monkey Dance is containment, de-escalation, and removal of the obstacle. It is not to win or make public anything.*
Pursuit Team Work for Important Opportunities *Page 146*	Configure the core team, which consists of people essential to the pursuit campaign. What areas of knowledge—again recognizing that knowledge consists of information and skill—are required to support team operations? Start with team leadership.
Team Mission Statement *Page 157-159*	The cornerstone to pursuit team focus and achievement is the mission statement. It consists of three main components and a number of subcomponents that every member of the core pursuit team will need to understand and personally internalize. Recognize that it's not a static document, but a living, changing, and dynamic expression of team purpose. This is the responsibility of the pursuit team lead, focusing on: 1. Sales Objective a. *What will be sold?* What are you selling and why?

Subject	Content
Continued from previous page	b. *When will it be sold?* c. *For what price?* Also note any performance-based revenue potential. 2. Extended Significance of this Deal to the Company a. *How will this deal produce future business?* b. *What does winning this deal mean to each pursuit team member?* 3. Point at Which Relative Superiority will be Achieved a. *Who is the likely primary competitor?* b. *At what point in time will a distinctive advantage be achieved over the competition?* c. *How will this be accomplished?*
Serving Clients *Page 161-163*	The pursuit team exists to serve the client and your company where serve means contribute to the client and your company in a manner worthy of trust. *It is not dictating to the client, nor is it accepting whatever the client wants from you.* • Serving the client should be done in balance with serving your company. Value to the client should be balanced over an appropriate timeframe with value to your company.

Subject	Content
Continued from previous page	Investing in and solving a client problem that is of commercial value to them, but not charging them for it or gaining some kind of value for your company violates fairness.

- The physical process of serving is to determine how to make a contribution to the client's business in a specific area, assess its value not from your point of view, but from the client's perspective, and then confirm that the service provided is in balance with the business interests of your company, in order to maintain fairness.

Sounds simple, but to accomplish this on a consistent basis requires leadership, strength, and confidence. Specifically, to tie all team factors together you must:

- Know your client as well as you know your company.
- Be ready, willing, and able to respectfully and diplomatically disagree with the client when you know by experience that what they are proposing is wrong, even though it is not what they want to hear. And be able to back up your position with credible facts.

Subject	Content
Continued from previous page	• Never communicate false information, omit information, or exaggerate anything that might mislead the client to any degree, directly or indirectly. • Never rationalize authority over the client. For example, if you're an industry leader it doesn't give you the right to be insensitive to client requirements when they don't align with your product and service strengths. Neither will you develop the view that the client should adapt its business to your solutions because your way is the right way. • Never rationalize professional desire over the client. That is attitudinally subordinating the client's priorities to your priorities where, for example, you work to force the client to make a buy decision before they are ready using pressure, fear, or false information. • Transparency should be encouraged whenever appropriate and reasonable, subject to confidentiality requirements, need to know, and professionalism, as considerations. • Always protect the integrity of your company's business. Be respectful and professional, but do not let a client "run your business," create inappropriate business risk, or compromise the financial condition of your company.

Subject	Content
Continued from previous page	• *Never allow any of your company executives, managers, or support people to go into the account and not comply with the above.* • *Never allow a company executive, manager, or support person to enter or interface with the account to address anything dispositive without the knowledge of the team lead.*
Customer Procurement Advisors *Page 172*	On the client buy side of large deals a new procurement advisor industry has evolved for all the reasons introduced earlier. *That said, the goal of the procurement advisor is not to manage the procurement process. He will do that by default, but his mission is to create significant business value for the buyer who is his client.*
Supplier Industry Advisors *Page 177*	On the sell side, the industry advisor is a rare breed, mainly because unlike the procurement advisor, she has both a formal and informal role that goes well beyond providing information on a specific industry. Certainly, she will understand all there is to know about an industry; what it is, what drives it in terms of market dynamics, emerging and existing trends, the major players, and so on. *But her goal is not to provide information. Her mission centers on knowledge, which*

Subject	Content
Continued from previous page	*consists of information and skills to produce increased business value for the client and competitive advantage for the supplier.*
Great Industry Advisors and Poem *Page 178, 179*	An exceptional industry advisor is one that goes beyond helping to resolve conflict after the fact but also works to resolve conflict before it ever happens. Operationally, this occurs when the industry advisor proactively ensures proper internal alignment within the supplier organization, between supplier and client, and between the supplier and the procurement advisor. It's all about keeping the pursuit team out of a Monkey Dance: *Going from good to great,* *Is getting ahead of the Dance.* *For when it's too late,* *The team has little chance.*
Seven Critical Thinking Points *Page 188-193*	For this reason and to assist you in going forward with important deal pursuits, the following seven critical thinking points are offered. They are limited to essential information only designed to direct and guide at a strategic level: 1. Define Important 2. Identify Potential 3. Get in Early

Subject	Content
Continued from previous page	4. Go or No Go. Qualify the potential opportunity. 5. Team Up. Configure the pursuit team and establish the necessary setup to ensure that it can operate effectively. 6. Close the Deal. When an important sales campaign is peaking and a decision is about to be made, explicitly close. This is a time for conviction and spirit: *It's the moment of truth,* *When closing a deal.* *Like that time in your youth,* *When you moved with zeal.* 7. Seek Wisdom
Selling and Mountaineering Emotion with the Mount Rainier Example *Page 196*	If you are a sales manager or an executive, think of yourself as a seller for a moment, imagine that you're climbing a mountain that symbolizes the customer. You've qualified the mountain in that conditions are good for the ascent from base camp, just as you would qualify an important opportunity. But unlike selling, if you make a mistake, you could die. On all but one of my climbs on Mount Rainier, they were preceded or

Subject	Content
Continued from previous page	followed by bodies being taken off the mountain. So, you begin your climb and make camp at the base of the upper mountain, which is steeper, harder, and way more dangerous than your climb so far on the lower mountain. But, you're there, just as is the case in being down selected on a key pursuit. In both cases the deck gets reshuffled with changing weather on the mountain and changes in the competitive landscape post down select.

Acknowledgements

This book reflects the insights that our team at Holden has discovered on the front line of driving business with clients. It is a no-holds-barred point of view on how bad culture is damaging businesses on a global level and what to do about it. This would not be possible without the trust and support of the clients we serve. Their confidence in us and the work we do for them has made this book possible.

Supporting our geometric approach to culture, looking at it from many different angles—particularly those involving scripture, mountaineering, medicine, special operations, industry specialization, and college life—are two contributors, Charlie Kirk and Rj Smith. Both are dear friends and patriots who excel in their dedicated professions with giving hearts. Their input is reflected in the great reviews that sit at the front of our book expressing the opinions of clients around the world. Our thanks go out to these incredible contributors and reviewers.

Equally, and of special mention, is Patrick Nicolet, who wrote the Foreword. He is without doubt one of the most intelligent and dedicated business practitioners that I have ever met, and it has been an honor and privilege to work with him over so many years.

Turning our focus inward, there is the core team at Holden of Paul Dillon, Mike Johnson, and John Cashman. They have not only contributed directly to the thinking in this book, but also live the book's point of view—its values and caring for people. They are the salt of the earth, and I'm honored to be among them as a friend and colleague. And, in that regard, the longest-standing member of our team is a business partner, friend, and my wife, Chris Holden, who has supported this effort and everything else in my life.

Turning the view upward, there is the source of wisdom and determination that fills the "soul" of this book with purpose and meaning. I and our entire team believe this work to be divinely inspired—to play whatever role He has in mind, not just to impact sales, but to serve the greater good by bringing His presence into business.